APPOINTED TIMES

APPOINTED TIMES

*An Urgent Message on the Future of this Generation
from Daniel's Prophecies*

Curtis H. Davis

VMI PUBLISHERS
Sisters, OR

Copyright © 2007 by Curtis H. Davis
Published in 2007

VMI PUBLISHERS

Published by VMI Publishers LLC
Camp Sherman, Oregon, 97730

ISBN: 9781933204352
Library of Congress Control Number: 2006936598

Author Contact: DavisCurtisH@aol.com

Printed in the United States of America

Cover design by Joe Bailen
Photo of the Author by Gary Brown

Dedication

This book is dedicated to my grandchildren,
Amanda, Kara, and Nathan,
and to all who will see these things come to pass in their lifetimes.

Acknowledgements

There may be no task more daunting than writing one's first book.
I am grateful to my wife, Lois, for being patient during the years of study and long hours of preparation of this volume, and for being a sounding board for the many ideas it contains.
I thank Melanie Stone for her help in organizing the materials in this book, and for deterring me from exploring those enticing peripheral issues during the development of this book.

Contents

The First "Little Horn," the Antichrist
The Second "Little Horn," Antiochus IV
Merger of Antiochus and Antichrist
From Obscurity to World Leader
The Antichrist in the Tribulation
    The Mark of the Beast
    The Religion of the Antichrist
    The World Domination of the Antichrist
    The Fate of the Antichrist

The Appointed Time in Hosea
The Prophet
    "Israel" and "Judah"
The Prophecy
    Fulfillment of the Prophecy
    Injuries to Israel
Can We Know the Time?
    Return of the Jews to God
Qualifiers to the Interpretation
Implications for the Contemporary Christian
Witnessing Faith

List of Illustrations

Preface

Many years ago I was asked to lead a group of college-age Christians in a home Bible study of the book of Revelation. I was a young professional pursuing a career, a deacon in our church, a teacher of an adult Sunday school class, and starting a family. Nevertheless, I accepted this opportunity with the confidence that I knew the subject well enough to prepare the materials a week or two ahead of the class, having grown up in a church where prophecy was taught regularly and where "prophetic conferences" were an annual occasion.

It was when I had to back up my lessons with the authority of the Scriptures that I realized that some of the things I had been taught were inconsistent to the point of being illogical. I struggled to make sense of them, became confused with the facts, and was very dissatisfied with my presentation of the materials. I am sure that the class was frustrated as well.

That experience led me to begin my personal search for an interpretation of end-time prophecy that would be consistent with all prophetic passages. I resolved that my only text would be the Bible and the only reference a concordance, with all other books and commentaries temporarily shelved. What I found to be more difficult was to unlearn some of the things I had been taught for almost thirty years while reconciling contradictions that arose during my study. I read the Scriptures over and over in different translations and took perceived problems to the Lord as one would consult with a mentor, laying out my confusions and understandings to the Father and asking how they should be resolved. To this day, it amazes me when I realize how the Holy Spirit patiently revealed my misconceptions and gave me the grace to change my thinking.

The ongoing study has given me a renewed conviction that the Bible is God's Holy Word, that He is in control of every aspect of the future, and an understanding that He had long ago determined the timing of those events. I am convinced that He will reveal those things even more clearly to the last generation of believers as the time of the end approaches.

It was not my intention to write a book as I undertook my study, but as I talked to friends and listened to the positions of others, both one-on-one and in the media, the need for documenting these ideas was reinforced in my mind. I then began to research a wide spectrum of eschatological thought to test whether my ideas would withstand reasonable challenges. For the most part, I have resisted the temptation to state the positions of others and then recite my arguments against them. Rather, I wanted to present the Biblical reasons for my conclusions, from which my answers to other theories are formed. I have also discovered some valuable supporting material, which I have included where it is relevant.

My prayer is that this book will guide the beginning student of prophecy through the Bible with the least speculation and a minimum of unanswered questions. The reader who may be familiar with another prophetic hypothesis is asked to study the material with an open mind, and then to prayerfully compare the relative merits of each. I encourage all readers to acknowledge the authority of the Scriptures, realizing that God's Word is infallible, while humans are not. I also encourage you to consistently ask the Holy Spirit to teach you God's Word on this specialized subject. I believe that He will then reveal mysteries to you, for our God is a loving God.

Introduction

I t is human nature to be interested in events that will affect you tomorrow, next year, or in years to come. Many watch newscasts or read the daily papers to learn what happened yesterday and what is planned for tomorrow, but only one source reliably tells us the destiny of the world. That source is the Bible.

About one-third of the Bible concerns prophecy, either the oracles of the prophets and how they were fulfilled, or how they will be fulfilled in the future. On two occasions Jesus said, "Heaven and earth will pass away, but My words shall not pass away." The first was when He delivered the Sermon on the Mount to a large number of His followers, explaining that He had come to fulfill the law and the prophets (Matt. 5:17-18; Luke 16:16-17). The second was in the Olivet Discourse, as He privately informed the disciples about the end times (Matt. 24:35; Mark 13:31; Luke 21:33). In both cases, He was assuring them of the sure word of prophecy, not just a portion of it, but every last word.

Daniel was told that in the latter days, there would be "those who have insight" who will give understanding to the people. You will see an increase of anointed preachers and teachers passing this knowledge on to their disciples as we approach the fulfillment of these things (Amos 3:7). When we know what will happen in the future, we can prepare ourselves for the time we will encounter them, while resting in the assurance that the One who will bring them to pass has the higher purpose of caring for those He loves.

You would not be reading this if God had not placed in you a desire to know His Word about things to come. You are not to wait for someone to tell you what the Word says, but to learn it for yourself. Some people avoid studying prophecy because it contains much figurative language and symbolism, and they consider it unfathomable or frightening. It need not be either. We will show you from Scripture that there is good reason to believe that He will return within the lifetime of many reading this book.

The purpose of this book is neither to complement nor to compete with Christian media commentators who try to identify current events with things prophesied in the Bible. We will not attempt to find traits of the coming "man of sin" in some contemporary personality so we can name the Antichrist. What we will try to do is to find the proper relationships of future events and put them in their proper time sequence so you will know more clearly, and with greater certainty, how God will wrap up the end of this age.

If this book helps you to understand God's plan for you, then we will have fulfilled our mission.

1

The Seventy Weeks
of Daniel

PRELIMINARY TO A HOLY VISITATION

By our calendar, the year was 539 BC. The aged man reclined in the opulent chambers befitting a member of the king's inner circle. He had been an official in the Babylonian government nearly all of his life and had been declared third in command only a few months ago. Ironically, it was on the night before a coalition of the Medes and Persians captured the city. A less civilized king would have put him to death, but Darius recognized Daniel's leadership qualities and retained him in high office. He also knew that having a respected Jew in a high position would help convince the growing number of his people to accept the new ruling order. It was another example of God's protection over His faithful prophet these many years.

On this particular day, Daniel was oblivious of the rich tapestries, the luxuriant rugs, the soft couches and the servants waiting silently just outside the door to attend to his slightest wish. He put down a scroll of smooth sheepskin that had been written by the prophet Jeremiah in Jerusalem. His faded memory of the Holy City was a prolonged backward look at the golden reflection of the rising sun on her walls and buildings as he was being taken into exile by the armies of Nebuchadnezzar. That was sixty-seven years ago, just after he had become *bar mitzvah*, "a son of the law." He had heard for years that the city and the temple of God were in ruins, a blight upon the land, and that many of those he had left behind had been killed or taken captive.

Daniel realized that what he had just read meant that his people would soon be allowed to return to the Holy City. But rather than feeling jubilant, he was troubled because he also knew that their exile and the destruction of Jerusalem were God's punishment, and that even after all these years, they had not really repented of their sin and neglect. He wondered if they were worthy to undertake the tremendous task of rebuilding the city, much less the sacred temple.

He put on a simple robe of sackcloth, the traditional garment of mourning, and wearily made his way to the window facing Jerusalem, to pour out his concern to God while confessing his sin and that of the people, and to ask God to look with favor upon the city.

As he was concluding his prayers, he sensed that someone was standing beside him (Dan. 9:4-19). Had he not given orders that he was not to be disturbed? Turning, he recognized Gabriel, the angel who years before had explained the meaning of a vision he had concerning future world rulers. The message Gabriel delivered that day concerned seventy "sevens" of years in which the future of Israel was revealed. It is as relevant to us as it was to Daniel.

THE MAN, DANIEL

Who was Daniel, and what personal characteristics qualified him in God's eyes to be the recipient of a major prophecy? His exemplary life is deserving of an in-depth study, and while several miracles with which he was associated are taught in Sunday school classes and are the basis of many sermons, we also want to take note of his devotion, humility, and obedience.

The Young Daniel
We don't know much about Daniel's childhood. He probably lived in Jerusalem with his parents and siblings all of his formative years. He certainly received the daily education to which each male Jewish child was

entitled and undoubtedly attended the temple services every Sabbath day. He would have had household chores to perform and played with simple toys his father made. A highlight of his adolescent life could have been the times that the prophet Jeremiah came to town bringing warnings of punishment from far away peoples if they did not repent of their neglect of God. These words probably shaped the young Daniel's thinking years later:

> From the thirteenth year of Josiah the son of Amon, king of Judah, even to this day, these twenty-three years the word of the Lord has come to me, and I have spoken to you again and again, but you have not listened. And the Lord has sent to you all His servants the prophets again and again, but you have not listened nor inclined your ear to hear, saying, "Turn now everyone from his evil way and from the evil of your deeds, and dwell on the land which the Lord has given to you and your forefathers forever and ever; and do not go after other gods to serve them and to worship them, and do not provoke Me to anger with the work of your hands, and I will do you no harm."
>
> "Yet you have not listened to Me," declares the Lord, "in order that you might provoke Me to anger with the work of your hands to your own harm. Therefore thus says the Lord of hosts, 'Because you have not obeyed My words, behold, I will send and take all the families of the north,' declares the Lord, 'and I will send to Nebuchadnezzar king of Babylon, My servant, and will bring them against this land, and against its inhabitants, and against all these nations round about; and I will utterly destroy them, and make them a horror, and a hissing, and an everlasting desolation.'" (Jer. 25:3-9).

One day in 606 BC, Daniel experienced the vindication of Jeremiah's words when the armies of Nebuchadnezzar swept in and plundered the city, even taking the gold utensils used in the temple offerings. Worse, they carried off to Babylon, "youths in whom was no defect, who were good-looking, showing intelligence in every branch of wisdom, endowed with understanding, and discerning knowledge, and who had ability for serving in the king's court (Dan. 1:4)." One of those youths was Daniel. We know the names of only three others caught up in that initial assault. In this first invasion, the Babylonians did not harm the land itself. But because the Israelites stubbornly refused to pay tribute, there were two more attacks, each ten years apart, and each more destructive than the one before it, until finally the city and the temple were burned and the walls torn down.

In Babylon, the boys were put into a three year re-education program to teach them the Babylonian language, customs, and skills to prepare them for personal service to the king. What would you imagine would be the destiny of teenage boys removed from the support and guidance of parents and priests, no longer able to attend religious services, and immersed in an exotic culture in the palace of a king? What were their chances of maintaining their Jewish distinction?

They passed their first moral test when they were required to eat the food of the palace, food and drink that were forbidden by Mosaic Law. Daniel asked that they be allowed to eat kosher meals, and the Bible tells us that they thrived mentally and physically to the glory of God (Dan. 1:10-16).

Less than a year after being taken to Babylon, Daniel was called upon to interpret a disturbing dream that God gave to the king (Dan. 2:1-45). God let Daniel see the same dream and gave him the interpretation, thus securing his position in the palace.

The Length of the Captivity

As Jeremiah had preached for twenty-three years, the people of Israel were to be punished for their idolatry and neglect of God, if they did not repent of their evil. He also said that the Captivity was to last seventy years. There are some who believe that this was to allow the land to rest for this specific length of time. Let me explain. When Israel entered the land promised to Abraham, they were told to work the soil for six years, but to allow the earth to lie fallow in the seventh, even as God rested on the seventh day of creation. The land would produce normally for five years, but in the sixth year, it would give them an abundant crop to tide them over the seventh year and provide seed for the eighth crop. They failed to trust the Lord in this matter for 490 years. Therefore, God would see that the land would get its sabbatical rest in one stretch of seventy years (Lev. 26:33-35; 2 Chron. 36:21; Dan. 9:11).

Daniel's Adult years

After the term of his apprenticeship was completed, he entered a profession that we would call "civil service." One has to wonder if God hadn't placed him in the higher levels of government to look out for the civil interests of his people. While we don't have any evidence that Daniel directly interacted with his countrymen, we know that Ezekiel lived among them and ministered to them. Jeremiah also wrote a letter to the exiles with words from the Lord about their captivity, instructing them to cooperate with their captors because they would be there for a long time. A portion of that letter reads,

> Thus says the Lord of hosts, the God of Israel, to all the exiles whom I have sent into exile from Jerusalem to Babylon, "Build houses and live in them; and plant gardens, and eat their produce. Take wives and become the fathers of sons and daughters, and take wives for your sons and give your daughters to husbands, that they may bear sons and daughters; and multiply there and do not decrease. And seek the welfare of the city where I have sent you into exile, and pray to the Lord on its behalf; for in its welfare you will have welfare" (Jer. 29:4-7).

Many years later, toward the end of the seventy year Exile, King Belshazzar hosted a drunken celebration, toasting the Babylonian gods using gold cups that had been removed from the Jewish temple years ago. When they had done so, a disembodied hand wrote the doom of the kingdom on the wall in a strange language, and when Daniel was able to translate the message, the king appointed him to the third highest position in the land (Dan. 5:16). Daniel said, in effect, "Give your rewards to someone else; this is the last day this kingdom will exist!" That night, the Medes and Persians diverted the river that flowed through Babylon and walked in under the gates that once protected the city from river invaders.

The new Medo-Persian king observed Daniel's skills and appointed him an executive over the commissioners and *satraps* in the new government. The jealousy of the others around him prompted them to lay a trap for him, resulting in Daniel spending the night with the lions, as you probably recall. He was then more than eighty years old (Dan. 6:1).

So Daniel lived the whole time of the exile in luxury, but keeping himself a pure vessel so that God entrusted him with a number of visions that he recorded for us.

Daniel's Visions

By the way the narrative of the Bible is written, people are inclined to think that prophets received one vision after another, with frequent visitations of angels. In Daniel's case, it was fifty years after the interpretation of King Nebuchadnezzar's dream that Daniel recorded a second vision (Dan. 7:1). His third came a few years after that (Dan. 8:1). Debatably, all of Daniel's visions came to him when there was a major change of gentile rulers over Israel.[1] The difference between those earlier visions and the one we are going to study is that this prophecy reveals *when* the things predicted would happen, and *how long* they would last.

Can something be too good to be true? This is apparently what some think about Daniel's visions; the prophecies recorded in his book were so accurate that skeptics say that he wrote them after they happened. In other words, they say that he was an historian rather than a prophet, but while the secular world may reject Daniel as a prophet, Jesus Himself gave him that recognition (Matt. 24:15). Moreover, the book of Daniel contains prophecies that were not fulfilled until 32 AD and 70 AD, long after the book had been placed in their synagogues.

The Prophecy of the Seventy Weeks

God is always receptive to hearing our prayers and more than willing to meet our needs, which He understands better than we do. In the first year of the Medo-Persian rule, Daniel read the book of Jeremiah and fell under great conviction. He prayed for forgiveness, not only of his sins, but the sins of his people. He asked for nothing other than that, but as he concluded this prayer, God sent "the man Gabriel" with what is arguably the most important message about the future of his people we have in the Bible.

Gabriel came to Daniel to give him "insight and understanding." Strong's concordance says that the root meaning of "insight [*sakal*] is "to be circumspect." The word for "understanding [*binah*]" means "to discern." Certainly that is what the Holy Spirit expects of you and me as we study this sacred text. The record of the vision follows, with my emphasis and commentary:[2]

Seventy "sevens" are decreed for your people and your holy city

- to finish transgressions,
- to put an end to sin,
- to atone for wickedness,
- to seal up vision and prophecy [prophet][3] and
- to anoint the most holy.

Know and understand this:

From the issuing of the decree to restore and rebuild Jerusalem until the Anointed One, the ruler [Jesus Christ] comes [as Messiah on Palm Sunday], there will be seven "sevens," [when the temple was restored] and sixty-two "sevens." It will be rebuilt with streets and a trench, but in times of trouble. <u>After</u> the sixty-two "sevens," the Anointed One [Jesus] will be cut off [crucified] and will have nothing [or no one]. The people of the ruler who will come [Antichrist] will destroy the city and the sanctuary. [Fulfilled by the soldiers of the Roman Empire on the 9th of the month Av, AD 70.]

> The end will come like a flood: War will continue until the end, and desolations have been decreed. He [Antichrist] will confirm a covenant with many for one "seven" [the final week], but in the middle of that "seven" he will put an end to sacrifice and offering. And one who causes desolation will place abominations on a wing of the temple until the end that is decreed is poured out on him (Dan. 9:24-27 NIV).

The word "week" is used in some translations, instead of the more accurate word "seven" as the NIV translates it. But since we are dealing with time, and since we English speaking peoples commonly use "week" for a group of seven days, it has become accepted by prophetic students to refer to a "week" of years in this context. History has confirmed that the "sevens" of this prophecy are sevens of years. Thus we have the term, "The Seventy Weeks of Daniel."

The year, as used for this prophecy, is certainly *not* our calendar year of 365 days with periodic leap years of 366 days. While the early Egyptians knew the length of a solar year with some accuracy, the Jews have always used a year of twelve months (from new moon to new moon), and starting about 500 BC, they inserted an extra month as necessary to align the calendar with seasonal events such as the barley harvest.[4] The prophetic year is neither of these.

Daniel was told plainly that the time allotted to the "ruler who will come" would be three and one-half years following the "abomination of desolation" (Daniel 7:25; 12:7). Other passages describe other future events of forty-two months or 1,260 days. They can only be reconciled if one uses a year of twelve months of thirty days each; therefore, we speak of a "prophetic year" of 360 days. We will examine the use of these various expressions in the Bible in the next chapter.

THE TIMING OF THE PROPHECY

God had set a precise appointed time for the prophecy to begin, and we will discuss the reason for that shortly. That time was "From the issuing of the decree to restore and rebuild Jerusalem," and the decree was one that was issued by King Artaxerxes in the Jewish month Nisan, in the twentieth year of his world supremacy (Neh. 1:3; 2:8, please read the context).

Some have confused this decree with another issued years earlier by King Cyrus, allowing Ezra and thousands of other Jews to return to Jerusalem to rebuild the temple of God (Ezra 1:1-4). But in their zeal to restore Solomon's temple that Nebuchadnezzar tore down, some of the Israelites started to do something that would have negated the letter of the prophecy. They began to work on the walls of the city.

Ezra had opposition to the work he was doing, and whether or not they knew that they were doing the will of God, their enemies reported the work on the walls back to Babylon, leading to the cessation of all work being done in Jerusalem (Ezra 4:12, 21). When the work resumed later under the direction of Zerubbabel, it was only the temple that was restored (Ezra 5:2).

In this manner were the Word of the Lord preserved and the prophecy of the seventy weeks begun on time.

THE FIRST SIXTY-NINE WEEKS

The seventy weeks are presented as groups of seven, sixty-two, and one, with a break before the last week (see the time line of figure 1-1). The Bible does not tell us what marked the end of the first seven weeks, but it almost certainly marked the completion of the rebuilding of the walls, gates, guard towers, water system, etc. in Jerusalem.

The Bible offers little information about events of the first sixty-nine weeks of years in this passage. The book of Ezra tells of the rebuilding of the temple, and Nehemiah records the problems and rebuilding of the infrastructure of Jerusalem in the first seven weeks. The period began with a decree from the gentile king Artaxerxes that allowed Nehemiah to restore and rebuild the walls and gates of Jerusalem (Neh. 2:5-7). This is not to be confused with earlier decrees of Cyrus and Artaxerxes permitting work on the temple (Ezra 1:1-4; 7:1-26).

Sir Robert Anderson, a nineteenth century lawyer and Scotland Yard inspector, wrote an important work in which he makes a compelling argument for a literal fulfillment of the first sixty-nine of Daniel's seventy weeks using a 360-day prophetic year.[5] He dates the start of the prophecy on 14 March, 445 BC with the decree by Artaxerxes allowing the Jews to rebuild the city (Neh. 2:1), and the end of the sixty-ninth week with Jesus' Triumphant Entry into Jerusalem on 6 April, AD 32, confirmed to the day. He further reconciles it with the calendar year of 365-1/4 days.[6]

That first "Palm Sunday" came a short time after Jesus raised Lazarus from the dead and healed others on His last journey to Jerusalem. The common people loudly proclaimed Him "the king who comes in the

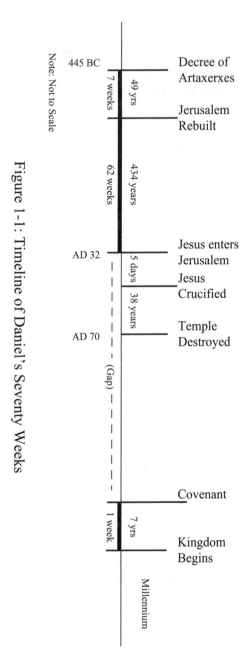

Figure 1-1: Timeline of Daniel's Seventy Weeks

Note: Not to Scale

445 BC — Decree of Artaxerxes

7 weeks | 49 yrs

Jerusalem Rebuilt

62 weeks | 434 years

AD 32 — Jesus enters Jerusalem

5 days | Jesus Crucified

38 years | AD 70 — Temple Destroyed

(Gap)

Covenant

1 week | 7 yrs

Kingdom Begins

Millennium

name of the Lord" as they escorted Him into the city. The Pharisees undoubtedly recognized the implications of what they were saying and told Jesus to rebuke them, but He replied that if these were to be silent, "the stones will cry out" (Luke 19:38-40). Why was it so important that Jesus be received as the Anointed One *on that particular day*? It was because that day, and none other, was God's appointed time for the fulfillment of Daniel's prophecy, and it could not be stopped or changed!

BETWEEN THE 69TH AND 70TH WEEKS

Anyone observing that the sixty-nine weeks were literally fulfilled might reasonably expect that the seventieth week would immediately follow, with the end of the age coming just seven years later and the whole prophecy completed in AD 39. But the prophecy also predicted two events that would take place following the sixty-ninth week. The first of these was that the "Anointed One" would be "cut off," and the second was that the city and sanctuary would be destroyed by "the people of the prince who is to come" (Dan. 9:26). Jesus was crucified only five days after the end of the sixth-ninth week, but it was thirty-eight years later that the city and temple were destroyed.

So it is evident that God ordained a break, or gap, between the end of the sixty-ninth and the beginning of the seventieth week, but there is nothing to indicate the length of the break. Some have described this as "the prophetic clock having been stopped (or put on hold)." Others have likened it to a train being shuttled onto a side track while the express train passes on the main track. The clock will resume its ticking or the train will be put back on the main track when the church fulfills the task it has been assigned. This author feels strongly that God has a set, appointed time for all things, and that He is not dependent upon us for anything before He can act. On the other hand, He knows what His people will do in the future, and this is reflected in what He has revealed to us in the prophecies.

There is a prophecy in Hosea that explains that the Jews will be abandoned by God for a period of time (Hosea 6:1-2). We will discuss this prophecy and its implications in the last chapter of this book. But God will not go without a witness for Himself in the interim, and that witness is the church He ordained. Paul describes the church as a wild Olive branch being grafted into the cultivated Olive tree of Judaism. Most call this period "The Church Age," although it started before the destruction of the temple, and will end before the Millennium (see figure 1-2).

The Anointed One Cut Off

After the conclusion of the sixty-ninth week, the Anointed One would be "cut off," a clear reference to the death of Jesus. He and His twelve disciples were in Jerusalem for Passover, an observance that has its roots in a ritual that was begun on the night before the Exodus. To avoid the death of the firstborn in the household, each family had to kill a lamb for a supper ritual and sprinkle its blood on the doorposts and lintel of the residence (Exod. 12:3-28). The death angel would see the blood and "pass over" that house.

The gospels say that Jesus went to Jerusalem that year specifically to deliver Himself into the hands of those who would put Him to death. Jesus is the lamb that died for our sins, and He is symbolized as such in the Revelation (Rev. 5:6). He lived a sinless life, and it is His blood that satisfies the requirement for forgiveness of sin. Have you acknowledged that He died for you?

Destruction of Jerusalem and the Temple

The other event that was predicted to take place after the sixty-ninth week was the destruction of Jerusalem and the Tabernacle by "the people of the prince that is to come (Antichrist)." This was fulfilled when the Roman general Titus and legions of Roman soldiers broke through the defenses of Jerusalem in August, AD 70 after two years of siege. Because of this reference, we have reason to believe that the Antichrist will be of Italian ancestry. We discuss this further in the Chapter, The Antichrist.

The Roman Empire had engulfed most of Europe and all of the lands around the Mediterranean Sea by the time Jesus was born. But even though Rome controlled Israel, they wisely let the Jews govern their own people in most day-to-day civil matters and they were allowed to worship in their temple and synagogues. Still, Roman soldiers were present every-where in the land. A soldier could demand that a citizen carry his burden for one mile, or to share their food and clothing with him. This was the reason why Jesus, in the Sermon on the Mount, told His followers that if they were compelled to carry a burden a mile, they should go two, and if a soldier demanded their shirt, they should also give him their coat. The Jews generally resented the Roman soldiers, and a radical band of nationalists, called zealots, now constituted a significant underground resistance. You may recall that one of Jesus' disciples was "Simon, the zealot" (Luke 6:15).

Under the enforced peace of the Roman iron fist, the church was born, missionaries sent out, and churches established in the Middle East, Asia Minor, and Europe. But arsonists burned most of the city of Rome to the ground in AD 64. Historians believe that the emperor Nero ordered the destruction because he considered himself to be a great archi-tect and civil engineer, and he wanted to rebuild the ancient city to his own design. He blamed the fires on the Christians, whom the Romans considered a sect of Judaism and a rapidly growing threat to the empire. You may have read about Christians who were put into the Arena to fight lions, or being sewn into animal skins and set upon by wild animals, or being crucified. Nero, in particular, would cover their bodies with tar, impale them on poles, and set them afire to illuminate his garden parties. A hatred of Jews and Christians spread to the outlying provinces like the fires spread throughout Rome. It was about this time that Paul and Peter were both martyred.

In AD 66, some Jewish zealots in Judea ambushed the Roman Royal Guard in a mountain pass, handing them a humiliating defeat. Two years later, a much larger and stronger Roman army returned to capture Jerusalem. The city fell on 9 Av (August 2), AD 70, and the temple burned. It was the anniversary of the destruction of Solomon's temple in 586 BC. After the fire, the Romans tore down the walls of the temple to get at the gold overlay that had melted and run between the stone blocks, thus fulfilling Jesus' prophecy that not one stone would remain upon another (Matt. 24:2).

Hundreds of thousands of Jews were slaughtered and a similar

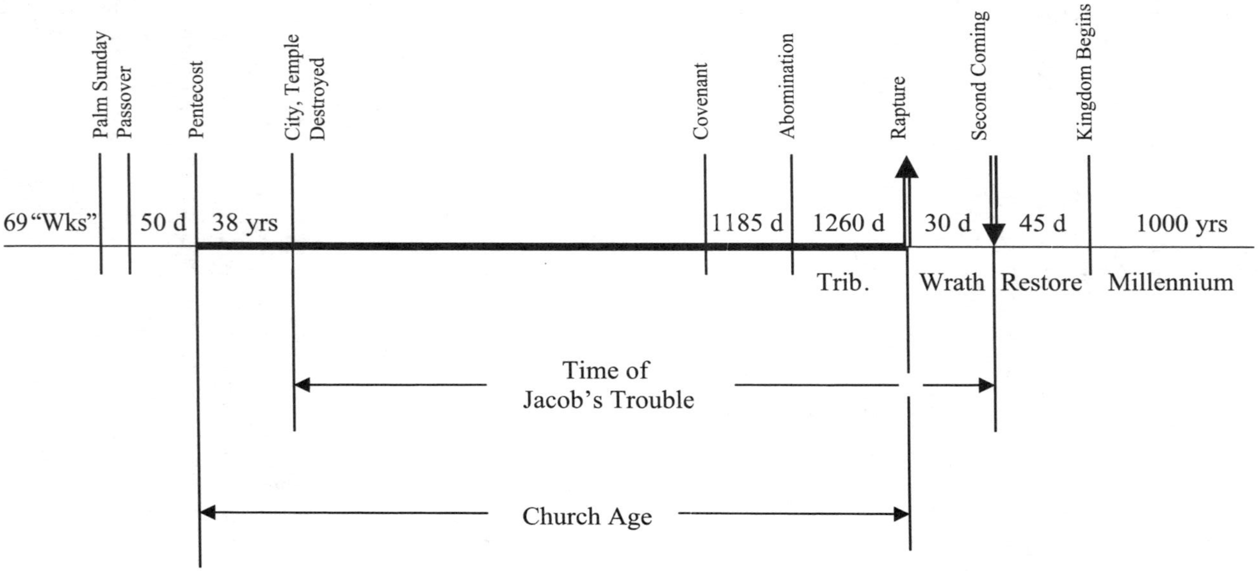

Note: not to scale

69 "Wks" — Palm Sunday
50 d — Passover
38 yrs — Pentecost

— City, Temple Destroyed

Church Age

Time of Jacob's Trouble

Covenant
1185 d
Abomination
1260 d
Trib.
Rapture
Wrath 30 d
Second Coming
Restore 45 d
Kingdom Begins
Millennium 1000 yrs

Figure 1-2: The Church Age

number sold into slavery. A small group of zealots held off the Romans for a few more years at a desert outpost called Massada. The rest fled to countries throughout the world. This is known as the *Diaspora* that the Jews mourn to this day. In the last days, all the Jews from all parts of the world will return to the land God gave to them thousands of years ago (Ezek. 39:28).

Thirty-eight years, five months elapsed from Palm Sunday until the destruction of the temple, and almost 2,000 years have passed since then. When will Daniel's prophecy resume with the seventieth week of years?

The Church Age

We often hear the time in which we are living called "The Church Age," which many equate with the period between the sixty-ninth and seventieth weeks of Daniel's prophecy. A little reflection upon church history shows us that this is not exactly true, although some may consider the distinction to be trivial.

First of all, there is no such designation in the Bible, which recognizes only "the present age" and "the age to come." It is at best, a convenient label we have attached to the time that God raised up a Holy Spirit filled body as His earthly witness in the absence of His chosen people. Most agree that the Church Age began at Pentecost (some will say it started at Calvary), which was always observed fifty days following Passover and thus fifty-six days after the end of the sixty-ninth week. The church lives into eternity, but since we are considering these ages from the perspective of those living on earth, the Church Age will end at the Rapture. The time of the Rapture is hotly debated by the proponents of different pre-millennial theories. Figure 1-2 shows the author's viewpoint of the Church Age relative to "The Time of Jacob's Trouble" (Jer. 30:5-7) and other events we will be discussing.

The Seventieth Week

In the next chapter, we will consider the seventieth week of the seventy week prophecy delivered to Daniel. It is covered by just one verse in

Daniel (Dan. 9:27), while Jesus left us a commentary on the week in Matthew 24-25, Mark 13, and Luke 17 and 21. Paul placed nuggets of information about the week in the epistles he wrote to churches he founded, especially the letters of 1 Corinthians and 1 and 2 Thessalonians. John wrote "The Revelation of Jesus Christ" as it was shown to him, in the same manner that Daniel was personally given visions by a heavenly messenger.

The twelfth chapter of Daniel introduces periods of thirty and forty-five days that follow the Tribulation. There are prophecies in the Old Testament and the Revelation that were not fulfilled in the sixty-nine weeks, nor do we find them in the Tribulation. The only period into which they can logically fit are those seventy-five days. A short list of these things is the Day of Christ, the Wrath of God, the second coming of Christ, Armageddon, the Sheep and Goat Judgment, the return of the Jews from other lands, and the renovation of the earth by fire in preparation of the Millennium. We believe this to be the Day of the Lord, and we address it in chapter three.

Daniel was told that the events of the last days would come as a flood, and the analogy is certainly apt. We have spent a brief chapter on 483 years; we will spend another on seven years, and yet another will cover just seventy-five days.

The Seventieth Week
of Daniel

We are living in an interesting, if not exciting, time! Twenty-six hundred years ago, God sent an angel named Gabriel to tell the prophet Daniel the future of the rest of this age as a span of sixty-nine weeks of years, followed by a gap of time, and then the final week of seven years. We are living in that gap, waiting for the final countdown. Everything in the first sixty-nine weeks, and even two significant events after the sixty-nine weeks, has taken place. We anticipate the resumption of the prophecy, expecting to see the things we know will take place, but wondering what else they will bring and how the rest of the world will react to them. We will discuss all but the last seventy-five days of that final week in this chapter.

The following is the portion of Daniel's prophecy of the seventy weeks that is still unfulfilled, with the author's comments:

"…The end will come like a flood [in rapid succession]: War will continue until the end, and desolations have been decreed. He [the ruler who will come] will confirm a covenant with many for one "seven" [the final week]. In the middle of the "seven" he will put an end to sacrifice and offering. And on a wing [extremity, edge] of the temple he will set up an abomination that causes desolation, until the end that is decreed is poured out on him" (Dan. 9:26b-27 NIV).

Embodied in these two short verses are all the end-time prophecies of the Old Testament, Jesus in the Olivet discourse, Paul and Peter in their epistles, and John in the Revelation. These two verses are the framework upon which all of the predictions of the end-times may be attached.

In these verses, Daniel succinctly affirmed a period of seven years defined by a covenant and marked in the middle by an abomination. A little later, he had another visitor from heaven who expanded upon what Gabriel said, telling him about the rise of "a despicable person" [Antichrist] to a position of strength (Dan. 11:21-28), his desecration of the temple and dominance over "people who know their God" (Dan. 11:31-35), his arrogance toward God, and his ultimate demise (Dan. 11:36-45).

This messenger (it could have been Gabriel) informed Daniel of a "time of distress" to come, the "rescue" of his people (the Rapture), and of a general resurrection of the dead (Dan. 12:1-3). The final verses of his book tell us how long the "time of distress" (Tribulation) will last, and introduce the thirty and forty-five day periods that would follow it (Dan. 12:4-13).

When that last week begins, the events will "come as a flood," that is, they will be overwhelming to those living on the earth, with each succeeding disaster impacting the world before the shock of the preceding one has had a chance to be absorbed. In this chapter, we will examine all but the last seventy-five days of "The Day of the Lord."

How the Week will be Divided

The brief message to Daniel quoted above made it clear that the Antichrist will violate the covenant in the middle of the week by causing the temple offerings to cease. What is meant by "the middle of the week"?

As we mentioned in the previous chapter, the years of this prophecy are 360 days long and the final week will consist of 2,520 days. The reference to "the middle of the week" has resulted in most interpreters dividing the week into two equal halves of 1,260 days each, but this has led to further disagreements. When we consider the numerous events that are said to be 1,260 days, forty-two months, or three and a half years long, do we assign them to the first half of the week, or the second? Your answer will shape your entire view of the end-times.

There is no reason for confusion or disagreement in this matter. What many have overlooked (or willfully ignored) is that Daniel was given additional revelation about the seventieth week that showed that the halves of the week will *not* be equal. He was told that there will be two brief, but significant, periods of time that follow a period of tribulation. The first will begin 1,260 days after the Abomination and end at 1,290 days, and the second begins at 1,290 days and ends at 1,335 days. Simple arithmetic says that if there are 1,335 days from the Abomination to the end of the week, there can be only 1,185 days from the covenant to the Abomination; therefore, we have the unequal halves.

Some might argue that, if the Abomination is closer to the beginning of the week than the end, it cannot be said to be in the *middle* of the week. However, the Hebrew word used for "middle" (*chatsi*) is an imprecise term that is found in Joshua 10:13 when the sun stood still in the "middle of the sky." It was the "middle of the night" in Ruth 3:8, and Zechariah 14:4 uses it to describe the Mount of Olives being "split in the middle" at the second coming of Jesus. The middle of Daniel's week does not have to be measured to the exact day, hour, minute, etc. to satisfy the meaning of the text.

All of this is to show that *there will be only ONE prophetic period of 1,260 days, forty-two months, or three and one-half years in the last week,* and that it begins with the Abomination. The first mention of this period was Daniel 7:25, in a vision of a "little horn" (the Antichrist), who will be given dominion over the saints for "time, times, and half time" (three and one-half years). That phrase is repeated in Daniel 12:7 and again in the New Testament to confirm that it will be the length of time that Israel will be sequestered in the wilderness to escape persecution by Satan (Rev. 12:14). But just a little earlier in that same chapter, the same event is said to last "1,260 days." Just one chapter before that, John was told that two witnesses will prophesy to the world for the same 1,260 days (Rev. 11:3). The term "forty-two months" is the time that the Gentiles will tread the Holy City (Rev. 11:2), and the time during which the Antichrist will be permitted to continue in power (Rev. 13:5). That

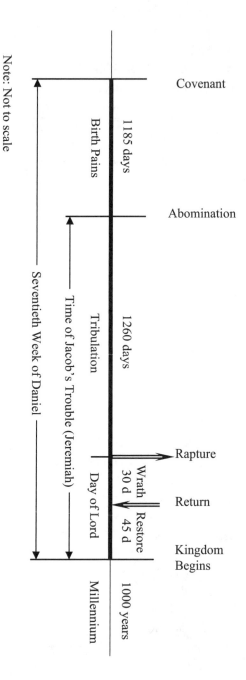

Figure 2-1: Timeline of Daniel's Seventieth Week

reference to his authority over the saints takes us back to Daniel 7:25 and the three and one-half years! So this very important period is expressed three different ways, and taken together, they describe the time we call "The Tribulation."

Other than being informed about the coming periods of thirty days and forty-five days, Daniel was not told what significance they hold for Israel. In fact, he was told that the meanings were sealed (closed up) until the time of the end. We, however, have two advantages that were not available to Daniel. First, we know from secular history which of his prophecies have already been fulfilled, and when. Second, other prophets tell us about a number of things that will take place in the last week. Therefore, we know what prophecies we may *exclude* from later fulfillment, and to some extent, when future events will take place relative to each other.

For those who appreciate a graphic representation of the end-times, figure 2-1 shows how we think these events will play out in the last seven years of this age.

THE COVENANT

"And he will make a firm covenant with the many for one week…" (Dan. 9:27)

The final week is defined when "he [the ruler who will come] will confirm a covenant with many for one seven." The passage is not one that is easily translated from the original Aramaic, as is evident by comparing differing English translations of the prophecy. However, they all agree upon the following facts:

- The term of the covenant will be seven years.
- The prince who will come (the Antichrist) will be one of *many* signatories of the document.
- Halfway into the period of the covenant, the empowered Antichrist will violate its provisions and render the temple unfit for sacrifice and worship.
- He will prevail until the end that God decreed for him is carried out.

I prefer the NIV to the NASB translation of this passage that uses the phrase "on the wing of abominations," or the KJV that reads, "Overspreading of abominations." We know from Matthew 24 that there will be one abominable image set up in the temple (Rev. 13:14-15). Many abominations will follow this defining act in the Tribulation.

For years, there has been one interpretation of the covenant that has dominated the teaching of the end-times to the evangelical community. That interpretation says that the globally powerful Antichrist will be one party of the treaty, and that the Jews are "the many" with whom the treaty is made. Not only is that interpretation strange for the document that the Bible describes, but it also begs the question, "Why would the Antichrist, who controls the world and hates the Jews with such great intensity, sign a peace treaty with them, and why would it have a specific time assigned to it?" Another problem with this theory is that the covenant is signed at the *beginning* of the week, while the Bible indicates that the Antichrist will not be revealed until the *middle* of the week,[7]

I propose a different explanation for why the covenant will be drafted. It seems almost certain that current tensions in the Middle East will escalate until Israel and her adversaries agree to a negotiated settlement drawn up by an organization like the United Nations or the European Union as a temporary seven-year solution while a permanent settlement is worked out.[8] This "resolution," as the United Nations would call it, will be signed by delegates from member nations (the many), and among them will be the man who will become the Antichrist. He will sign the covenant as the Bible says, but he will not be revealed at that time as the one who will eventually violate it, except to the one who does some research, such as getting a list of signatories to identify our suspect.

The treaty will not be exclusively with Israel, because the nations that surround Israel also have to agree with its provisions. It is often called a "peace treaty," and certainly the purpose of formal agreements like this one is to provide a groundwork wherein all parties can live peacefully with mutual understanding, but the Bible does not call it anything but a covenant. The activities of the Antichrist described in Daniel 11:21-45 and the birth pains that Jesus described in the Olivet discourse testify to the fact that there will not be global peace to celebrate.

Based upon issues that are important in the first decade of the twenty-first century, there will be at least two main provisions that the covenant must address. One is that the Palestinian Arabs be given a territory with a capitol in Jerusalem. The other is that the Jews will be permitted to build a temple on that piece of land known as the "Temple Mount." The document will almost certainly contain numerous other provisions, such as disarmament, surrender of lands, exchange of prisoners, reparations, etc.

The temple must be built on the precise spot as the first two temples, and the altar must be placed on the spot where Abraham intended to sacrifice Isaac (Gen. 22:1-18).[9] At this time, no one knows the exact location of that place with certainty, but the general wisdom has been that it is a sizable rock outcropping over which the Islamic "Dome of the Rock" was built. The Muslims call it "*es sakhra*," to commemorate the place they say that Mohammed ascended into heaven. For the Jewish temple to be built on that site, the mosque would have to be destroyed. This is unthinkable in the minds of many, but some radical groups have been caught with the ways and means to do just that.

The reader should be aware that there is no unanimous agreement that that site is the correct one. One source has identified twelve authorities with different ideas about where the temple was situated, relative to the Dome of the Rock.[10]

One proposition is that the place where the altar rested is a second location where the native rock is exposed through the paving blocks, about a hundred meters (one football field) north of the mosque and directly in line with the eastern gate through which the Messiah will enter when He returns to earth.[11] According to Hal Lindsey in a broadcast of his "International Intelligence Briefing," a new temple of the size required by the Pentateuch could be built on that site without encroaching upon the Islamic mosque. Any such temple would be highly controversial, even with the force of a treaty behind it, and groups of zealots and individuals would surely try to sabotage the work, even at the risk of sacrificing their lives.

Luke's account of the Olivet discourse includes a statement that Matthew omitted, "When you see Jerusalem being surrounded by armies, you will know that its desolation is near" (Luke 21:20). Matthew wrote, "Therefore when you see the abomination of desolation which was spoken of through Daniel the prophet, standing in the holy place (let the reader understand), then let those who are in Judea flee to the mountains…" (Matt. 24:15-16). These comments need not be mutually exclusive. He probably made either statements at one time or another during this discussion with the disciples. The appearance of armies around Jerusalem soon after the covenant is signed would be an indication that trouble could arise (Luke), but the abomination would be a sign that distress for the Jews was about to take place (Matthew).

If the covenant will be administered by the United Nations or similar agency as we have proposed, armies consisting of member nations would be deployed to enforce its terms, and those armies could be commandeered by the Antichrist on short notice once he achieves world domination by the middle of the week. The fact that Jesus warned the Jews not to return to their homes when they see the Abomination suggests that their oppressors will already be present in Jerusalem when it is set up.

Jesus gave the Abomination in the middle of the week as the sign that the disciples asked for as evidence that Jesus' coming and the end of the age is near (Matt. 24:15). Although the covenant will be signed years before the Abomination, it was not presented as the sign they asked for, which implies that the covenant will not be generally recognized for the important role it plays in eschatology. However, people who know the Bible will recognize the covenant for what it is, and will probably try to warn others of the important period they will be entering. There may be reports about those crazy Christians who think that the end of the age is near, but the media will trot out Bible "experts" to deny that it has any significance and tell those concerned that Daniel was not a "true" prophet. Nevertheless, the covenant will almost certainly be celebrated by the world as a brilliant document that will assure a solution to the Middle East conflict, and any protest will be quickly silenced.

THE FIRST HALF OF THE WEEK

And he will make a firm covenant with the many for one week,
but in the middle of the week he will put a stop to sacrifice and
grain offering (Daniel 9:27).

Some theories define the entire seventieth week of Daniel as the
tribulation, but the term "tribulation" does not describe the situation of
the Jews for the first half of the week, when they will be protected by the
covenant and the Restrainer has not yet released the Antichrist to make
war against the saints (Rev. 13:5-7). In the Olivet Discourse, Jesus said
that the tribulation comes after the "birth pains," that is, after the
Antichrist declares himself to be God.

The Beginning of Birth Pains

Using the metaphor of a woman in labor, Jesus characterized the first half
of the week as "the *beginning* of birth pains." In the last days of preg-
nancy, contractions signal that the time to deliver is at hand. The birth
pains are generally mild at first, but they become more frequent and grow
more intense until the birth. After the covenant, but before the
Abomination, you may expect a few skirmishes to escalate into many,
and localized struggles to become ferocious battles.

  The first thing Jesus told His disciples was that they would hear of
wars and rumors of wars, implying that Israel herself will not be involved
in them. It will not be so for the rest of the world. Crops will be ruined
or not planted, resulting in widespread famines. Strange plagues will
spread geometrically and even the most wealthy nations will not be able
to cope with the problems on a global scale.

  If these are the *beginning* of birth pains, then what are the "hard"
birth pains? I propose that they are seen in the Trumpet Judgments of the
Tribulation and the Bowl Judgments of the Wrath of God of the *second
half* of the seventieth week. What is given birth is the physical kingdom
of God in the age that immediately follows.

Events Leading Up to the Abomination

"The abomination of desolation" is the singular event that unambiguously introduces the Antichrist to the world and starts the countdown of the 1,260 days of the Tribulation to the Day of Christ. How does he rise from an obscure military officer or politician to the position of a world leader? We will leave most of the details for our chapter on the Antichrist, but for now we recognize that he first becomes the leader of his own country through skill, bribery, and miraculous intervention before he begins to conquer other nations (Dan. 11:22, 26). At some point, probably close to the middle of the week, he suffers a mortal wound, but is raised from the dead. The people of the world will give Satan credit for the miracle and worship the resurrected man saying, "Who is like him?" (Rev. 13:3-4). Thus there will be a deification of a secular ruler. This is almost incomprehensible to the Western mind, but fully ingrained in Middle Eastern and Far Eastern cultures.

Nevertheless, the world will see his resurrection and subsequent demonstrations of power performed on his behalf, which will result in a great apostasy of professing Jews and Christians. Heady with the adulation he receives, and with the Restrainer no longer holding him back, he will "sit in the temple of God, showing himself to be God" (2 Thess. 2:3-4).

The Restrainer

Satan was jealous of God even when he was in heaven as Lucifer, the angel of light. He would like us to worship him and control our lives, but the Bible tells us that there has also been a person called "The Restrainer," who has been holding him back. The Restrainer is the Holy Spirit, but a time is coming when He will be taken out of the way (He is not "taken out"), allowing the Antichrist to reveal himself and begin to exercise his authority to a degree he had not been permitted before. The work of the Restrainer will be concerned as much with preventing the Antichrist from revealing himself before his appointed time as it will be restricting his power. But from the moment he claims to be God, he will focus upon deceiving all who are not saved through signs, false wonders, and wickedness. God will assist him by sending a deluding influence upon every one who has not received the love of the truth so they might believe what is false and be judged (2 Thess. 2:6-12). Those familiar with the Scriptures will be awed by what they are seeing, but they will not be deceived.

The Apostasy

The act of apostasy is defined as "an abandoning of what one believed in, as a faith, etc."[12] It could apply to the truly saved or to the merely professing individual, but the person who has never claimed to believe in God cannot be called an apostate. The root word in Greek means "defection" or "revolt," and has been translated "a falling away (from the faith)," "desert," "withdraw," or "depart." Some have taken the latter definition to suggest that Paul was talking about a departure from the earth in the Rapture rather than a defection from a professed belief, but there is no hint in the context that this was his intended meaning.

> Let no one in any way deceive you, for it will not come unless the apostasy [falling away—KJV] comes first, and the man of lawlessness is revealed, the son of destruction," (2 Thess. 2:3).

> But the Spirit explicitly says that in later times some will fall away [depart—KJV] from the faith, paying attention to deceitful spirits and doctrines of demons," (1 Tim. 4:1).

Christians today tend to think of the apostasy only in terms of the church, but it applies to Jews as well. The Antichrist will reward those who forsake the Mosaic covenant (Dan. 11:30). Considering the culture of modern churches in the Western Hemisphere, it will surely involve the unsaved who attend church solely for social and economic benefits. When *professing* believers see the signs and wonders of the two witnesses also being performed by the False Prophet on behalf of the Antichrist, they will readily cross over to the side of the Man of Sin. They should know better, but they will fall under that deluding influence we spoke of earlier. Lest you think that the appeal of the Antichrist will be trivial, I remind you that Jesus said that even the elect would be deceived, *if that were possible* (Matt. 24:24). The scope and breadth of the rebellion against God will contribute to the hatred, betrayal, and murder of family members that Jesus said would characterize the last days (Matt. 24:9-10; Mark 13:12-13; Luke 21:16).

THE ABOMINATION OF DESOLATION

And on a wing of the temple he will set up an abomination that causes desolation (Daniel 9:27 NIV).

Up to now, we haven't said much about the False Prophet, who seems to hold a subordinate position to the Antichrist, but who will do the work that focuses the world's attention upon him and exalts him as an object of worship. He will have two close associates (the two horns he is said to have). It is he who will set up the Abomination in the temple (The Beast from the Land, Revelation 13:14-17), who also gives the image its breath and the ability to speak. The Old Testament says that it will be set up by "forces from him (the despicable man" (Dan. 11:31)).

The Antichrist inflicts two insults upon the temple. One is the time he sits in the temple to proclaim himself as God (2 Thess. 2:3-4), and the other is when his image defiles the temple (Dan. 11:31; Matt. 24:15; Mark 13:14). The Bible doesn't tell us which comes first, but it is logical that the image will be erected to commemorate the act of the Antichrist declaring himself to be God. The Abomination is clearly the image in the temple, and it is prefigured in Daniel 8:11, mentioned in Daniel 9, 11, and 12; Matthew 24; Mark 13; Revelation 13; and alluded to in 2 Thessalonians 2.

At this time, there is no temple in Jerusalem to be desecrated, so it must be constructed for this prophecy to be fulfilled. The current political situation in Israel makes any Jewish worship at the temple site impossible, but the covenant may provide the means, time, materials, manpower, and money for the temple, or at least the sanctuary, to be built in the first half of the week. Some groups are even now gathering materials necessary to build the temple and perform ritual sacrifices, including the red heifer required for the sanctification of the building, utensils, and priests (Num. 19:2-10). On October 13, 2004, seventy-one Rabbis re-formed the body of the Sanhedrin for the first time in over 1,600 years.[13] Among other things, this body has authority over all things pertaining to the temple, sacrifices, or touching in any way upon religious law.[14]

Do you doubt that the temple could be built so quickly? After all, King Herod worked on his temple for a half century. There are two Greek words that are translated "temple" in the New Testament. One (*hieron*) included the entire temple complex including the sanctuary, outer courts, and other buildings, while the other word, used in connection with the Abomination, designated only the sanctuary (*naos*).

It is also possible that a mere tabernacle (tent), such as the one David pitched over the ark, could be quickly erected to serve the purpose of offering sacrifices (2 Sam. 6:17). Maybe this is why Jesus said at this point, "Let the reader understand" (Matt. 24:15), or to paraphrase, "you must discern the nuance of this subject to master it."

Gentile readers may wonder why we are spending all this time telling them what will happen to the Jews in the end-time. We must keep in mind that when Jesus instructed the disciples on the Mount of Olives, there was no church, and while the earliest church was largely made up of Jews (by lineage), the church in the end-times will very likely consist of mostly gentile believers. There is a verse at the end of the allegory of the Woman and the Dragon that has chilling relevance to the church. "And the dragon was enraged with the woman, and went off to make war with the rest of her offspring, who keep the commandments of God and hold to the testimony of Jesus" (Rev. 12:17). Jews do not "hold to the testimony of Jesus." Only the church fits this description, and this verse tells us that Christians will also be targets of Satan's wrath.

THE SECOND HALF OF THE WEEK

...and on the wing of abominations will come one who makes desolate, even until a complete destruction, one that is decreed, is poured out on the one who makes desolate (Dan. 9:27).

The abomination of desolation signals the beginning of the persecution of those who worship the one true God. There are two places in the Bible that tell of an *unprecedented* time of tribulation or distress for God's people (Dan. 12:1-2; Matt. 24:15-21). Since both passages claim a unique level of persecution, we may conclude that Daniel and Jesus referred to the same event.

When we study the Olivet discourse, we will see that Christians will be hated for the name of Jesus in the Tribulation, either because they honor His name, or simply because He was a Jew. That hatred will permeate all nations, so there will be no place on earth where they will be welcomed. False prophets will rise up to deceive the unsaved, and many who formerly professed to believe in Jesus will turn away from the faith. Believers will be turned over to the authorities by their own brothers, sons and fathers to be persecuted and put to death. The love (goodwill or affection) of many will grow cold. It was in this context that Jesus told them that they should not prepare their defense before being arrested, but simply to allow the Holy Spirit to speak through them (Matt. 24:9-14; Mark 13:9-13; Luke 21:12-19).

But while Christians and Jews will be persecuted for their love of God, we should not read the Tribulation judgments of Revelation as their punishment. Like the ten plagues upon Egypt in Moses' day, the punishment will be upon those who persecute the righteous (Exod. 5-12). The Abomination will serve as a warning for the Jews to go into hiding, and it will be the marker from which the duration of other prophetic events will be measured (Dan. 9:27; 11:31; 12:11).[15]

Many of the events of the Tribulation are found as obscure references in prophetic passages of the Old Testament. The struggle of Israel with Satan is found in the metaphor of the Woman and the Dragon in Revelation 12, which includes their preservation of the Woman in the wilderness. Revelation 14 tells the story through a series of angelic appearances. God's response to the persecution of His people is described in the trumpet judgments of Revelation.

Antichrist's World Domination

With the Restrainer no longer holding him back, the Antichrist, "whose coming is in accord with the activity of Satan" (2 Thess. 2:9), is free to resume his agenda of world domination and the elimination of any who worship the true God. His specific activities are described in Daniel 11 and Revelation 12 and 13. Much of the latter Scriptures are figurative, but what he does must be interpreted as being literal. We are told that his influence is global:

> "And the great dragon was thrown down, the serpent of old who is called the devil and Satan, who deceives the whole world; he was thrown down to the earth, and his angels were thrown down with him" (Rev. 12:9).

> And I saw one of his heads as if it had been slain, and his fatal wound was healed. And the whole earth was amazed and followed after the beast; (Rev. 13:3).

> …for they are spirits of demons, performing signs, which go out to the kings of the whole world, to gather them together for the war of the great day of God, the Almighty (Rev. 16:14).

Do not read these verses to mean that every person on earth will follow the Antichrist and take his mark. He will be globally renowned, and although he may have disciples in every nation on earth, he may be dominant in some of them, and not so strong in others. The Bible tells us that there will be many that will *not* be deceived, including the righteous of the "sheep and goats judgment" (Matt. 25:31-46) and the Jews who will come through the testing and enter the Kingdom (Zech. 13:8-9).

> And all who dwell on the earth will worship him, everyone whose name has not been written from the foundation of the world in the book of life of the Lamb who has been slain (Rev. 13:8).

> And those who dwell on the earth will wonder, whose name has <u>not been written</u> in the book of life from the foundation of the world, when they see the beast, that he was and is not and will come (Rev. 17:8).

> If anyone's name was <u>not found written</u> in the book of life, he was thrown into the lake of fire (Rev. 20:15).

The Mark of the Beast

The program for the Mark of the Beast is found in just one passage of Scripture, although there are six other references in Revelation that describe the destiny of those who take the mark.

> And he [the beast from the land] causes all, the small and the great, and the rich and the poor, and the free men and the slaves, to be given a mark on their right hand, or on their forehead, and he provides that no one should be able to buy or to sell, except the one who has the mark, either the name of the beast or the number of his name. Here is wisdom. Let him who has understanding calculate the number of the beast, for the number is that of a man; and his number is six hundred and sixty-six (Rev. 13:16-18).

God put His mark on select people on at least three occasions, and it was always for their protection. The first was Cain, who was afraid that his own life would be taken by others when they found out that he had killed his brother Abel (Gen. 4:14-15). The second is a fascinating story found in Ezekiel 8 and 9, when God revealed to Ezekiel the wickedness of the priests and elders, and then told an angel to mark the foreheads of those who had not engaged in idolatry. The death angel was told to kill anyone who did *not* have the mark. The third occasion will be the sealing of the 144,000 in the forehead with the names of God and Jesus (Rev. 7:2-8).

Satan is a jealous imitator of many of the things that God has instituted for mankind. In the end-times, he will devise an unholy trinity by equating himself as God, the Antichrist as Son (including his death and resurrection), and the False Prophet as the Holy Spirit. When God commissions two witnesses in the Tribulation, Satan gives the False Prophet two assistants (his two horns). And when God seals the 144,000 for their protection, Satan comes up with his own seal, the Mark of the Beast.

Not all people will bow to the Antichrist when he declares himself to be God, so the False Prophet devises a plan to compel their worship. He will have men create an image [*eikon*, a likeness] of the Antichrist and erect it in the temple. We are not told how large it will be or of what it will be made, but we know that the False Prophet will give it the ability to speak. Voice recognition and synthesis are technologies now available to us, and I'm guessing that the image will probably be very sophisticated, and probably interactive; that is, it will be able to respond spontaneously to questions and instructions.

All men and women will be required to swear devotion to the Antichrist [we aren't told to what extent children will be involved]. They will be given a choice of being tattooed [the Greek word means a *scratch* or an *etching*] in the forehead or right hand. I can imagine that devoted followers will have the mark put prominently where it can be seen by all, whereas the more reserved may have it placed on the hand. The many Jews and Christians who flee when the Abomination is put in place will not take the mark, and will have to depend upon God to provide for them, just as He preserved Israel in the exodus from Egypt. In the metaphor given to John, it is said that Israel will be *nourished* in a hiding place for 1,260 days (Rev. 12:6, 14).

Every person must have the mark in order to engage in commerce. If you want a loaf of bread, you go to a grocer, who will probably have the mark on his forehead, you show him yours, and the food is purchased in a routine transaction. Those without a mark will have to buy on a black market [I assume there will be those in most places], or get help from a sympathetic friend or neighbor having the mark. If he tries to buy anything, he will be turned away or possibly reported to the authorities. The alternative is to starve, if you are not being nourished by God in the wilderness.

It is a simple, inexpensive, and effective concept. No paperwork or computer need be involved. The mark will be the same for everyone, and it will be the name of Antichrist or his number, 666.[16]

Merely getting a tattoo does not bring the wrath of God upon an individual. What is abhorrent to God is the fact that one must worship or swear allegiance to the Beast to receive the mark (Rev. 14:9-11, 16:2, 19:20, and 20:4). God is jealous of being the one true God, and He will not share that with any other.

We are a people who tend to be awed by technological advances. Seventy years ago, the mark was believed to be just what the Scriptures describe, but as new technologies were developed, ideas about the fulfillment of prophecy changed as well. In my lifetime of more than six decades, I have heard the claim that the mark would be one's Social Security number (SSN), in spite of the fact that Scripture says that it will be the same for all people and that the SSN is restricted to the United States. When inks were developed that could only be seen under ultraviolet light, it was imagined that the SSN would be imprinted, but invisible. With the advent of computers, claims were made that the Antichrist would electronically store our personal data in a huge database, and the list of information he would demand expanded as the density of memory improved. Pictures of people with barcodes on their foreheads began to surface when the Uniform Product Code (UPC) was devised. The latest iteration of the myths about the mark involves a wireless chip under the skin.

As an electronics engineer of many years, I could give you several reasons why the concept of a tiny implanted chip for real time global positioning and data exchange is unrealistic at this time, but the thing to remember is that these ideas go far, far beyond anything the Bible said the mark must be. Those who believe in the imminent return of Christ should simply reflect upon the fact that neither the technology nor the infrastructure to support this program is in place at this time.

The concern we should have about these distortions is that some sincere people could be deceived when the program of the mark is in place. Yes, they should know better than to worship the Antichrist in any manner, but if they believe that the mark will be an implanted electronic chip, they might not object to having a simple tattoo put on the hand.

The Two Witnesses

The only significant opposition the Antichrist will have during the Tribulation will be two divinely appointed witnesses who will minister during the time that the Antichrist will be empowered. They will have the ability to call down fire from heaven to kill anyone who tries to harm them. They can demand that it will not rain, turn the seas to blood, poison the fresh waters, or call any plague they wish at any time they wish and as often as they wish (Rev. 11:6). The powers they have are the same as those described in the first four Trumpet Judgments. In that regard, the trumpets may be the proof of the witnesses' authenticity.

Now here is the rub. The False Prophet of Revelation 13 will also be able to work miracles, and specifically to call down fire from the sky. By performing the same signs and wonders as the two witnesses, he will deceive the world into choosing the Antichrist over the real Messiah.

Many of the saints and Jews will be in hiding and protected from these things, but the Scriptures also say that multitudes will be martyred during the Tribulation. The deaths of the two witnesses will be the final blow that leaves the righteous with no strength (power or influence). If Satan would be permitted to have dominion over the saints for more than the allotted time, no Jew or Christian would remain alive to take part in the Rapture (Mark 13:20).

Precisely three and one-half days before the end of the 1,260 days, the Antichrist will be permitted to kill the witnesses. Their burial will be denied and their bodies left lying in the street, while the scene will be flashed in real time to the world by satellite television, picture phones and the internet, to fulfill the prophecy that the whole world would look upon them. Considering that the two witnesses had created drought and plague and called down fire, the people of the world will believe that they will finally be safe from these two troublemakers. They will rejoice over their deaths and send greetings and gifts to one another in a short-lived celebration.

The Angelic Shout—The Resurrection

The Bible says that, "While they [the world] are saying, "Peace and safety!" then destruction will come upon them suddenly like birth pangs upon a woman with child; and they shall not escape" (1 Thess. 5:3). On the 1260th day, the breath of God will enter the witnesses, and they will rise to their feet. Their decaying bodies will be instantly transformed to a state of incorruption. A loud shout is heard, "Come up here!" and the witnesses ascend to meet the Lord in the clouds. I believe that the shout heard here is the same one that Paul tells us will accompany the Lord in His Coming (1 Thess. 4:16). Paul told the Corinthian church that Jesus was the firstfruits of the Resurrection, and that "all that are Christ's" would experience the same transformation when He returns for His own (1 Cor. 15:20-23). I take that to mean that everyone of all time who benefit from the atoning death of Christ will be included in that resurrection and transformation; not just the church, but all of the Old Testament dead as well.

The Last Trumpet—The Rapture of the Living

The descriptions of Christ's coming all include the sounding of the trumpet of God. When the last trumpet of judgment is blown, the living Christians, whose names are written in the Book of Life, will be raptured and receive new, incorruptible bodies "in the twinkling of an eye." The enemies of Christ will witness a very visible demonstration of His power on that day, as Jesus and the heavenly hosts harvest the saints, dead and living, preparing for the next prophetic act.

> And the seventh angel sounded; and there arose loud voices in heaven, saying, "The kingdom of the world has become the kingdom of our Lord, and of His Christ; and He will reign forever and ever."
>
> And the twenty-four elders, who sit on their thrones before God, fell on their faces and worshiped God, saying, "We give Thee thanks, O Lord God, the Almighty, who art and who wast, because Thou hast taken Thy great power and hast begun to reign. And the nations were enraged, and Thy wrath came, and the time came for the dead to be judged, and the time to give their reward to Thy bond-servants the prophets and to the saints and to those who fear Thy name, the small and the great, and to destroy those who destroy the earth."

And the temple of God which is in heaven was opened; and the ark of His covenant appeared in His temple, and there were flashes of lightning and sounds and peals of thunder and an earthquake and a great hailstorm (Rev. 11:15-19).

This is how Paul described it:

Behold, I tell you a mystery; <u>we shall not all sleep, but we shall all be changed, in a moment, in the twinkling of an eye, at the last trumpet</u>; for the trumpet will sound, and the dead will be raised imperishable, and we shall be changed. For this perishable must put on the imperishable, and this mortal must put on immortality. But when this perishable will have put on the imperishable, and this mortal will have put on immortality, then will come about the saying that is written, "Death is swallowed up in victory" (1 Cor. 15:51-54).

For the Lord Himself will descend from heaven with a shout, with the <u>voice of the archangel</u>, and with the <u>trumpet of God</u>; and the <u>dead in Christ shall rise first</u>. Then we who are alive and remain shall be caught up together with them in the clouds to meet the Lord in the air, and thus we shall always be with the Lord (1 Thess. 4:16-17).

And the words of Jesus:

…and then the sign of the Son of Man will appear in the sky, and then all the tribes of the earth will mourn, and they will see the Son of Man coming on the clouds of the sky with power and great glory. And He will send forth His angels <u>with a great trumpet </u>and they will gather together His elect from the four winds, from one end of the sky to the other (Matt. 24:30-31).

The Rapture ends the Tribulation but not the seventieth week of Daniel; there are seventy-five days and many prophecies to be fulfilled before Jesus hands the Kingdom over to the Father (1 Cor. 15:23-24).

The Day of the Lord

The visual media has depicted the end of the world as a huge explosion, either from man's foolish handling of nuclear materials or a catastrophic phenomenon such as a collision with an object from outer space. The student of the Bible knows that this is fantasy of the mind, because earth will eventually be the home to an everlasting kingdom.

In many passages of both the Old Testament and the New Testament, the prophets describe horrific things in an event called "The Day of the Lord." It, too, will not be the end of the world, but it will be the end of "the present age," with the promise of a better age to come for those who have a proper relationship with God. Those who have not been reconciled with God have every reason to be in absolute dread of the Day of the Lord, but the good news is that no one *has* to be subjected to the wrath to come.

Sixty-nine of the seventy weeks of Daniel's prophecy were put behind us almost two thousand years ago, and technology, theology, geology, biology, and politics have come to the point that the last week could soon be fulfilled. The last few verses of Daniel's book mention the last seventy-five days of the week, but tell us little about their substance or significance. I believe that period to be "The Day of the Lord," which is described graphically and cryptically in many other places in the Bible.

THE TIMING AND DURATION OF THE
DAY OF THE LORD

You may ask why the Day of the Lord is placed at this particular time of the seventieth week, when others equate it with the Great Tribulation or even the entire seventieth week of Daniel. Some claim that we are even now living in that Day. Evidence in the Bible tells us where it belongs.

Timing relative to the works of Satan

The Day of the Lord will be preceded by a great apostasy and the revealing of the Antichrist when he sits in the Jewish temple and claims to be God.

> Now we request you, brethren, with regard to the coming of our Lord Jesus Christ, and our gathering together to Him, that you may not be quickly shaken from your composure or be disturbed either by a spirit or a message or a letter as if from us, to the effect that the day of the Lord has come. Let no one in any way deceive you, for it will not come unless the apostasy comes first, and the man of lawlessness is revealed, the son of destruction, who opposes and exalts himself above every so-called god or object of worship, so that he takes his seat in the temple of God, displaying himself as being God (2 Thess. 2:1-4, cf. Matt. 24:10).

Paul also associates the Day of the Lord with the Rapture in this passage ("our gathering together to Him"). He is not equating the two, but implies that the Day of the Lord and the Rapture happen almost simultaneously. Neither is he saying that the Day of the Lord begins with the apostasy or the revelation of the Antichrist, but that these two things are precursors of the Day. We believe that the Apostasy is a result of the death and resurrection of the Antichrist, and that the Antichrist will reveal his true nature shortly afterwards, toward the middle of the week.

Timing relative to the Two Witnesses

The two witnesses for God will call for disasters to strike the earth during the Tribulation, including drought, plague, fire from heaven, and water polluted with blood (Rev. 11:3-6). You can imagine the anxiety and disturbance in the world's population, who will not know what each morning will bring.

> Now as to the times and the epochs, brethren, you have no need of anything to be written to you. For you yourselves know full well that the day of the Lord will come just like a thief in the night. While they are saying, "Peace and safety!" then destruction will come upon them suddenly like birth pangs upon a woman with child; and they shall not escape. But you, brethren, are not in darkness, that the day should overtake you like a thief (1 Thess. 5:1-4).

When will the unsaved be proclaiming "Peace and Safety" to each other? There is only one time in the whole Tribulation that they will have reason to expect that their lot will improve, and that is when the two witnesses that tormented them with the plagues of the Trumpet Judgments are finally killed by the Antichrist. They will be so elated they will exchange gifts and greetings in celebration of their deaths (Rev. 11:7-10).

The Lord's coming shares two characteristics with a thief; it will be sudden, and it will be unexpected. How could Paul say that the Day of the Lord will come as a thief, and in the next breath tell the saints that they will not be overtaken by it? It was because the element of surprise belongs to the world, not to the one who knows the facts of the Bible. Sadly, it will also be a surprise to some Christians as well. (Read again the counsel to the church at Sardis in Revelation 3:3.) It should not be a surprise to those reading this book.

Timing relative to the Celestial Signs

Joel said it first, and Peter quoted him hundreds of years later in a sermon before the crowds in Jerusalem, saying that there would be distinctive signs in the heavens at the start of the Day of the Lord (Joel 2:31). Specifically, the Sun will become as dark as looking through a burlap bag and the moon will take on a blood-red color.

> "And I will grant wonders in the sky above, and signs on the earth beneath, blood, and fire, and vapor of smoke, the sun shall be turned into darkness, and the moon into blood, before the great and glorious day of the Lord shall come. And it shall be, that everyone who calls on the name of the Lord shall be saved" (Acts 2:19-21).

Jesus told the disciples about these celestial signs in the Olivet discourse when He linked them with His own coming at the end of the age.[17]

> But immediately after the tribulation of those days THE SUN WILL BE DARKENED, AND THE MOON WILL NOT GIVE ITS LIGHT, AND THE STARS WILL FALL from the sky, and the powers of the heavens will be shaken, and then the sign of the Son of Man will appear in the sky, and then all the tribes of the earth will mourn, and they will see the Son of Man coming on the clouds of the sky with power and great glory. And He will send forth His angels with a great trumpet and they will gather together His elect from the four winds, from one end of the sky to the other (Matt. 24:29-31).

The same phenomena that herald the coming of Jesus are those that Joel said would announce the Day of the Lord. His Coming follows "the tribulation of those days"; therefore, the Day of the Lord will likewise follow the Tribulation. It cannot both *follow* the Tribulation, and at the same time also *be* the Tribulation.

Timing relative to the Renovation of the Earth

Since Adam and Eve relinquished the stewardship of the Garden of Eden to Satan by their disobedience regarding the forbidden fruit, the consequences of sin have left their evidences in, on, and above the world. You see the results of sin everywhere you look. There is an urgent need for a new heaven (atmosphere) and a new earth, and God has promised that He will provide them for the Millennium. This cleansing, or restoration, must be the last thing that God does in this age, after the battle of Armageddon is fought, the Antichrist is thrown into the fiery lake, Satan is confined to the abyss, the "goats" of the Sheep and Goats Judgment are burned up, etc. This Restoration comes at the end of the Day of the Lord as we have defined it.

> (Jesus)…whom heaven must receive until the period of restoration of all things about which God spoke by the mouth of His holy prophets from ancient time (Acts 3:21; Rom. 8:20-23).

The Length of the Day of the Lord

It is generally agreed that use of the word "day" does not always demand a twenty-four-hour cycle of light and darkness. It is an expression that we still use frequently to indicate a period of time more properly associated with the substance of an event than to its duration. A person or a group may be said to have their "day" when they are empowered, exalted, and honored, as in a parade, a wedding, or a sporting event. The "Day of the Lord" is the time when God finally releases the check on His anger, to destroy His enemies and restore the damage they have done to His creation.

If the Day is not a twenty-four-hour period, just how long will it be? For the reasons listed above, and because the Day of the Lord is more often spoken of as a time of destruction and punishment, I choose to believe that it begins immediately following the Rapture when God pours out His wrath on the world in the Bowl Judgments, and that it ends when the earth has been cleansed and prepared for the Kingdom. Being somewhat of a dispensationalist, I view the Day of the Lord as the very last divine action of the present age, not a part of the Kingdom, and not an age of its own. Paul may have been talking about both the end of the Day of the Lord and the end of the age when he wrote: "then comes the end, when He delivers up the kingdom to the God and Father, when He has abolished all rule and all authority and power (1 Cor. 15:24).

The duration of the Day is probably the least significant of the discussions we could have about it, being of little consequence to our fundamental beliefs.

DAY OF THE LORD, DAY OF CHRIST, DAY OF GOD

The phrase, "Day of the Lord," is frequently found in the prophetic books of the Old Testament and has become a generic term for all cataclysmic end-time events. It follows, and does not include, the period we call "The Tribulation." How could a time during which Satan is empowered be any part of the Day of the Lord?

"The Day of the Lord" is also found in the New Testament, but so are "Day of Christ," and "Day of God." How one perceives these terms to relate to each other in purpose and timing determines, in part, how end time events are viewed.

"Day of the Lord" is found in Acts 2:20; 1 Corinthians 5:5; 2 Corinthians 1:14; 1 Thessalonians 5:2; 2 Thessalonians 2:2; and 2 Peter 3:10 where the Greek word *kurios* (master) is consistently used for "Lord." "Day of God (*theos)*" is found only in 2 Peter 3:12 and Revelation 16:14. "Day of Christ (*christos)*" is used exclusively in the letter to the Philippians and may have developed in that congregation as a synonym for the Rapture.[18] The letters to the Corinthian church mention "the Day of the Lord Jesus" in related Scriptures.

The Day of Christ and the Day of the Lord

It is my opinion that the whole purpose of the Day of Christ is to exalt the Lord Jesus before His enemies and detractors when He comes to redeem those who have entrusted their eternal destiny to Him. He will appear with the brightness of His glory to split a sky dimmed by a blackened sun so that every eye will be drawn upward to see Him whom they have denied and watch the saved being assembled in their glorified bodies by the Lord of Glory. He will bring the souls of saints long dead with Him so they can receive their new bodies and join those who are alive at His coming (1 Thess. 4:14). While it is often said that the Rapture will take place in the twinkling of an eye (1 Cor. 15:52), that is not a true representation of what the verse says. It is the *translation* of the old flesh to a new spiritual body that is said to be done in a very brief moment. The rapture of all the saints around the globe may be conducted more deliberately and with prolonged "presence" to honor the One by whom it is performed.

If you take the verses that use the proper name "Christ," "Christ Jesus," "Lord Jesus," "Lord Jesus Christ," and substitute the word "Rapture" or "Resurrection" where appropriate, the texts lose no meaning or significance. The events of the Day of Christ describe things that we would expect to be accomplished at the Rapture.

(Lord Jesus Christ)…who shall also confirm you to the end, blameless in the day of our Lord Jesus Christ (1 Cor. 1:8).

I have decided to deliver such a one to Satan for the destruction of his flesh, that his spirit may be saved in the day of the Lord Jesus (1 Cor. 5:5).

…just as you also partially did understand us, that we are your reason to be proud as you also are ours, in the day of our Lord Jesus (2 Cor. 1:14).

For I am confident of this very thing, that He who began a good work in you will perfect it until the day of Christ Jesus (Phil. 1:6).

…so that you may approve the things that are excellent, in order to be sincere and blameless until the day of Christ; (Phil. 1:10).

…holding fast the word of life, so that in the day of Christ I may have cause to glory because I did not run in vain nor toil in vain (Phil. 2:16).

In each of these passages, it is when the day of Christ finally arrives that the living Saint can be secure in the knowledge that he or she will not betray the trust of the Lord. Compare these with the words, "that the proof of your faith, being more precious than gold which is perishable, even though tested by fire, may be found to result in praise and glory and honor at the revelation of Jesus Christ" (1 Pet. 1:7).

None of the above verses describing the Day of Christ directly link them to the Day of the Lord. However, when Paul instructed the Corinthian church on the matter of handling a reprobate, he described some of the same things in the Day of the Lord Jesus that he attributed to the Day of Christ (see 1 Corinthians 5:5, above).

As we pointed out earlier, Paul said that the Christian would not be taken by surprise at the Day of the Lord, even though it comes upon the unregenerate as a thief in the night. That would be a very strange thing for him to say, if Christians had *already* been removed in the Rapture, as some say. It is clear that Paul knew that Christians would be on the earth to witness the beginning of the Day of the Lord.

> For you yourselves know full well that the day of the Lord will come just like a thief in the night. But you, brethren, are not in darkness, that the day should overtake you like a thief; (1 Thess. 5:2, 4).

> …that you may not be quickly shaken from your composure or be disturbed either by a spirit or a message or a letter as if from us, to the effect that the day of the Lord has come (2 Thess. 2:2).

Simple logic tells us that, if the Christian is present at the Day of Christ and will also see the Day of the Lord, then the two must occur virtually simultaneously, even though one focuses upon the person and work of Christ and the other upon the wrath of the Heavenly Father. (Note also that both are characterized by the sun being blackened and the moon appearing as the color of blood.)

The Day of God and the Day of the Lord

While the Day of the Lord and the Day of Christ have different objectives, it would appear that the Day of the Lord and the Day of God is one and the same thing. Peter treats them interchangeably.

> But the <u>day of the Lord</u> will come like a thief, in which the heavens will pass away with a roar and the elements will be destroyed with intense heat, and the earth and its works will be burned up. Since all these things are to be destroyed in this way, what sort of people ought you to be in holy conduct and godliness, looking for and hastening the coming of the <u>day of God</u>, on account of which the heavens will be destroyed by burning, and the elements will melt with intense heat! (2 Pet. 3:10-12).

If the Day of the Lord results in the elements being destroyed by fire, and if we find the Day of God described the same way, we can logically assume that they are the same thing.

Likewise, the gathering of the nations for the battle of Armageddon, associated with the Day of the Lord in the Old Testament, is equated to the Day of God in the New Testament.

> Hasten and come, all you surrounding nations, and gather yourselves there. Bring down, O Lord, Thy mighty ones. Let the nations be aroused and come up to the valley of Jehoshaphat, for there I will sit to judge all the surrounding nations. Multitudes, multitudes in the valley of decision! For the day of the Lord is near in the valley of decision (Joel 3:11-12, 14).

> …for they are spirits of demons, performing signs, which go out to the kings of the whole world, to gather them together for the war of the great day of God, the Almighty (Rev. 16:14).

To summarize, The Day of Christ is a time that the Lord Jesus will be exalted before the whole world, and the crowns He collects are the multiplied millions of the Dead in Christ and the raptured saints. The

Day of Christ is either the very first event of the Day of the Lord, or it immediately precedes it with heavenly signs. However, The Day of God appears to be simply another name for The Day of the Lord.

Order of Events in the Day of the Lord

Figure 3-1 graphically shows which events the Scriptures associate with the Day of the Lord, placed in the order in which I believe they occur. This forms the outline for the balance of this chapter, with substantiating evidence:

THE FIRST THIRTY DAYS

The Wrath of God

In the first pages of this chapter, we presented scriptural evidence to refute the notion that the entire seventieth week of Daniel's prophecy will be The Day of the Lord. The four passages we cited show that the Day of the Lord must follow the Tribulation and the Rapture and thus support the idea that the Day is the seventy-five day period at the end of the seventieth week.

Another common fallacy that needs to be disproved is that the Tribulation is the Wrath of God. While it is true that the Bible says that Believers will not be subject to wrath, the wrath from which we are immune is referring to something other than the 1,260 day Tribulation. We will further show that the more severe Wrath of God (notice the capitalization), although a part of the Day of the Lord, is also not the Tribulation. The fact that many of the church will be subject to the rule of Antichrist in the Tribulation does not mean that they are under the wrath of God. To the contrary, experiencing the Tribulation will be the means by which many will be "purged, purified, and refined" to His glory (Dan. 12:10).

Greek words for wrath and anger

There are two Greek words for wrath (or anger) in the New Testament. The one used more often is *orge* [vengeance, ire, justifiable abhorrence, or punishment]. I am sure that we each experience this form of anger in ourselves almost daily in reaction to something or someone that offends us. This is anger that is held in check, and ideally, it passes quickly without being detected. A more severe type of anger is *thumos* [passionate fierceness evidenced by hard breathing]. A tight closing of the fists, teeth clenched, eyes wide, face flushed, and a deep, heaving breath characterize this type of anger. It often results in some kind of physical action being taken. Both words are used of God in the New Testament, but it is *how* and *when* they are used that provides the basis of our argument. The differences would have been obvious to a person fluent in the Greek language.

The wrath of God that we shall escape

We understand from the above definitions that God's wrath is complex. It covers a spectrum of emotions and is expressed in a variety of circumstances. Chapters one and two of the book of Romans gives us a background for this study, first saying that mankind has an inherent knowledge of the existence and nature of God; but despite that, he has ignored God's instructions and insists upon indulging in gross sin. In that passage, it says three times that God has "given them over" to their sin, that is, He has passively allowed men to suffer the natural consequences of their disobedience. This is the minimal expression of God's anger, but it has led the unregenerate to charge God with not caring for those who ultimately reap the fruit of their own behavior, generally expressed in statements such as, "If there is a God, why is there so much suffering (disease, poverty, etc.) in the world?".

Another level of God's wrath, and the one most commonly mentioned in the New Testament, is the wrath of God that condemns a man or woman to hell. It is the wrath that does not immediately punish offenses, but takes notice of them for future reckoning. These are sins that are covered by the Blood of Jesus, if only the sinner would appropriate the atonement of His sacrifice.

>...because of your stubbornness and unrepentant heart you are storing up wrath for yourself in the day of wrath and revelation

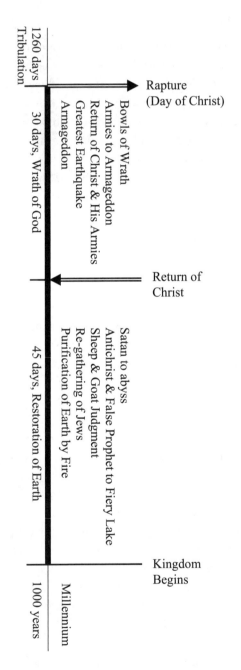

Figure 3-1, The Day of the Lord

1260 days
Tribulation

Rapture
(Day of Christ)

Bowls of Wrath
Armies to Armageddon
Return of Christ & His Armies
Greatest Earthquake
Armageddon

30 days, Wrath of God

Return of
Christ

Satan to abyss
Antichrist & False Prophet to Fiery Lake
Sheep & Goat Judgment
Re-gathering of Jews
Purification of Earth by Fire

45 days, Restoration of Earth

Kingdom
Begins

1000 years

Millennium

of the righteous judgment of God, who will render to every man according to his deeds: to those who by perseverance in doing good seek for glory and honor and immortality, eternal life; but to those who are selfishly ambitious and do not obey the truth, but obey unrighteousness, wrath and indignation (Rom. 2:5-8).

This is the fact that many miss when it comes to the *orge* wrath of God. In virtually every instance where it is found in the New Testament, it refers to the ultimate punishment of the unsaved in hell, as contrasted with salvation. It is not referring to the agenda of the Tribulation, nor to the next example of God's wrath.

For God has not destined us for wrath, but for obtaining salvation through our Lord Jesus Christ (1 Thess. 5:9 [see also Matt. 3:7; John 3:36; Rom. 1:8; Rom. 5:9; Eph. 5:6; Col. 3:6; 1 Thess. 1:10, 2:16]).

The Wrath of God in the Bowl Judgments

Thumos anger is far too common in mankind. Christians are admonished to identify it and to purge it from their lives (2 Cor. 12:20; Gal. 5:20; Col. 3:8). It describes the anger of Satan when he was cast out of heaven (Rev. 12:12). It is said to be the irrational anger that Pharaoh felt when Moses took the Hebrew children out of Egypt (Heb. 11:27). God's anger is characterized as the *orge*, or controlled anger in the New Testament, until we get to the Bowls of Wrath and the metaphor of the grapes of wrath found in Revelation 14 onward. Wherever the grapes of wrath or the winepress of His wrath are mentioned, God's anger is described as the *thumos* type. Interestingly, there are two verses where *both* expressions for wrath are found together for emphasis. There they are translated "fierce wrath" to show an extraordinary level of emotion (Rev. 16:19; 19:15).

The *orge* wrath of God therefore refers to the condemnation of sin, while the *thumos* wrath speaks exclusively to the punishment of the Bowl Judgments for those who have rejected His offer of salvation (Rev. 15-16) after the church has been removed at the last trumpet (Rev. 11:18).

It is seen metaphorically in the harvest of the wicked for punishment following the harvest of the saints for salvation.

> And I looked, and behold, a white cloud, and sitting on the cloud
> was one like a son of man, having a golden crown on His head,
> and a sharp sickle in His hand. And another angel came out of
> the temple, crying out with a loud voice to Him who sat on the
> cloud, "Put in your sickle and reap, because the hour to reap has
> come, because the harvest of the earth is ripe." And He who sat
> on the cloud swung His sickle OVER the earth; and the earth was
> reaped.
> And another angel came out of the temple which is in
> heaven, and he also had a sharp sickle. And another angel, the
> one who has power over fire, came out from the altar; and he
> called with a loud voice to him who had the sharp sickle, say-
> ing, "Put in your sharp sickle, and gather the clusters from the
> vine of the earth, because her grapes are ripe." And the angel
> swung his sickle TO the earth, and gathered the clusters from
> the vine of the earth, and threw them into the great wine press
> of the wrath of God. And the wine press was trodden outside
> the city, and blood came out from the wine press, up to the
> horses' bridles, for a distance of two hundred miles (Rev.
> 14:17-20).

The man or woman who has appropriated the forgiveness of sin
through Jesus will not be subject to the eternal *orge* punishment that
awaits the unrepentant, because he or she possesses the promise of salvation. But neither will the Christian living in the end time be subjected to
the *thumos* punishment of the Wrath of God in the Day of the Lord.
Neither principle, as wonderful as they are, promises the Saint protection
from the influence of the Antichrist in the Tribulation.

> And he [the Antichrist] will speak out against the Most High and
> wear down the saints of the Highest One, and he will intend to
> make alterations in times and in law; and they will be given into

his hand for a time, times, and half a time (Dan. 7:25 [See also Rev. 13:5]).

ARMIES ASSEMBLED AT JERUSALEM

When the sixth bowl of God's Wrath is poured out upon the earth, three evil spirits from Satan, the Antichrist, and the False Prophet go to the nations with miracles and persuasive speech to assemble the armies of the world to Armageddon, where they believe that they will take Jerusalem and defeat the Jews. They err in that they do not believe the promise of Jesus' Second Coming.

Jerusalem was, is, and will be a target for the enemies of the Jews. Shortly after the deaths of Paul and Peter, Jerusalem was besieged by four Roman legions that destroyed the city and the temple in AD 70. Daniel first received the substance of this truth in the prophecy of the seventy weeks, and Jesus repeated it just before He entered the city for the last time (Luke 19:41-44). Jerusalem was also attacked in the *Bar Kokhba* revolt of AD 132-135. Afterward, the Romans wanted to permanently desecrate the temple site by building a pagan temple on the site of the Jewish temple. The Muslim "Dome of the Rock" mosque now sits on that site.[19]

The city will be surrounded by armies in the seventieth week on at least two occasions. In Luke's account of the Olivet discourse, Jesus warned the disciples about armies surrounding the city at some time before the Abomination. We speculated earlier that these armies may be under the command of the United Nations to enforce the terms of the covenant signed at the beginning of the week.

> But when you see Jerusalem surrounded by armies, then recognize that her desolation is at hand. Then let those who are in Judea flee to the mountains, and let those who are in the midst of the city depart, and let not those who are in the country enter the city; because these are days of vengeance, in order that all things which are written may be fulfilled. Woe to those who are with child and to those who nurse babes in those days; for there will

be great distress upon the land, and wrath to this people, and they
will fall by the edge of the sword, and will be led captive into all
the nations; and Jerusalem will be trampled under foot by the
Gentiles until the times of the Gentiles be fulfilled (Luke 21:20-
24).

After the Tribulation, Jerusalem will again be under attack. The
Revelation account mentions Armageddon and Megiddo but not
Jerusalem itself. We learn that from Zechariah's account that Jerusalem will
be the target of their attacks before the Lord returns in the Second Coming.

Behold, a day is coming for the Lord when the spoil taken from
you will be divided among you. For I will gather all the nations
against Jerusalem to battle, and the city will be captured, the
houses plundered, the women ravished, and half of the city
exiled, but the rest of the people will not be cut off from the city.
Then the Lord will go forth and fight against those nations, as
when He fights on a day of battle (Zech.14:1-3).

Three prophets record the fact that armies of the nations gather at
Armageddon, and that they are there because God summoned them
there to punish them. This is John's text:

And the sixth angel poured out his bowl upon the great river, the
Euphrates; and its water was dried up, that the way might be prepared for the kings from the east. And I saw coming out of the
mouth of the dragon and out of the mouth of the beast and out
of the mouth of the false prophet, three unclean spirits like frogs;
for they are spirits of demons, performing signs, which go out to
the kings of the whole world, to gather them together for the war
of the great day of God, the Almighty. ("Behold, I am coming like
a thief. Blessed is the one who stays awake and keeps his garments, lest he walk about naked and men see his shame.")…And
they gathered them together to the place which in Hebrew is
called HarMagedon (Rev. 16:12-14, 16).

RETURN OF JESUS WITH HEAVENLY ARMIES

The classic post-tribulation theory teaches that Christ will appear in the clouds to catch up the church, only to return to *terra firma* immediately for the events of the Second Coming.[20] A study of the Revelation account seems clear on the point that the Bowl Judgments take place between those two aspects of His coming. The Bowls are the most intense form of God's Wrath upon those that have not acknowledged the Son of God as their Savior, including unrepentant Jews. It is the climactic event of the two days of the prophecy of Hosea 6:1-2 and the end of "The Time of Jacob's Trouble." Some say that this is the time of the Judgment Seat of Christ to reward the saints, but given their number, there is not enough time to properly judge them.[21]

With the armies of Satan gathered in one place (the sixth bowl), it is time for the Lord Jesus to come with the armies of heaven to battle with them. This is the Second Coming, when Jesus physically returns to the earth.

> A sound of the uproar of kingdoms, of nations gathered together!
> The Lord of hosts is mustering the army for battle.
> They are coming from a far country
> From the farthest horizons,
> The Lord and His instruments of indignation, to destroy the whole land.
> Wail, for the day of the Lord is near!
> It will come as destruction from the Almighty.
> (Isa. 13:4-6 [see also Isa. 34:1-6 and Joel 2:1-2, 11]).

> For I will gather all the nations against Jerusalem to battle, and the city will be captured, the houses plundered, the women ravished, and half of the city exiled, but the rest of the people will not be cut off from the city. Then the Lord will go forth and fight against those nations, as when He fights on a day of battle (Zech.14:2-3).

And I saw heaven opened; and behold, a white horse, and He who sat upon it is called Faithful and True; and in righteousness He judges and wages war. And His eyes are a flame of fire, and upon His head are many diadems; and He has a name written upon Him which no one knows except Himself. And He is clothed with a robe dipped in blood; and His name is called The Word of God. And the armies which are in heaven, clothed in fine linen, white and clean, were following Him on white horses (Rev. 19:11-14).

SHAPING THE EARTH FOR THE MILLENNIUM

The Old Testament describes the landscape of Israel as it will be in the Kingdom, and it is definitely not what you would see if you were to go there today. For example, the mountain upon which Jerusalem sits will be elevated while other mountains around it are leveled and the valleys between them will be lifted to create a plain upon which the Israelites will reside (Zech.14:8-10; Isa. 2:2; 40:4). Since the Millennium immediately follows the seventieth week of Daniel, the events that bring about these changes have to occur in the last half of the seventieth week.

We know, for example, that on the 1260th day after the Abomination, when the two witnesses are raised from the dead, an earthquake hits the region that kills 7,000 people and levels a tenth of Jerusalem (Rev. 11:13).

But even more devastating than that will be the earthquake that comes thirty days later, when Jesus sets foot on the Mount of Olives in the Second Coming:

And in that day His feet will stand on the Mount of Olives, which is in front of Jerusalem on the east; and the Mount of Olives will be split in its middle from east to west by a very large valley, so that half of the mountain will move toward the north and the other half toward the south (Zech. 14:4).

In another place, John recorded his vision of upheavals of the earth in more remote areas, with the timing seemingly coincident with the Second Coming:

And the great city [Rome?] was split into three parts, and the cities of the nations fell. And Babylon the great was remembered before God, to give her the cup of the wine of His fierce wrath. And every island fled away, and the mountains were not found. And huge hailstones, about one hundred pounds each, came down from heaven upon men; and men blasphemed God because of the plague of the hail, because its plague was extremely severe (Rev. 16:19-21).

Let me give you something further to think about. This is pure speculation on my part. The Mount of Olives is due east of the Temple Mount. The valley formed by the split of the Mount of Olives, extending east and west, will surely have to also split the Temple Mount. If the temple will be located north of the Dome of the Rock as we have proposed, the valley would create a chasm between the two, physically separating the temple from the mosque.

THE FINAL FORTY-FIVE DAYS (RESTORATION)

The first thirty days of the Day of the Lord end with the second coming of Christ. Another forty-five days of restoration and renovation are necessary to prepare the earth for the Millennium. Satan will be thoroughly defeated, but the debris and evidence of thousands of years of his dominion need to be eradicated on a new earth with a new atmosphere.

DESTRUCTION OF THE NATIONS' ARMIES (ARMAGEDDON)

When Jesus returns for the restoration of the earth, His first task will be the messy detail of dispatching the armies of Satan, who have conveniently gathered themselves together at Armageddon. The Bible metaphor for this confrontation is that of grapes being gathered at harvest time and thrown into a large vat to be crushed. In those days, and even today in some parts of Europe, the juice of grapes is pressed out by walking on them with bare feet.

> Let the nations be aroused and come up to the valley of
> Jehoshaphat,
> For there I will sit to judge all the surrounding nations.
> Put in the sickle, for the harvest is ripe.
> Come, tread, for the wine press is full;
> The vats overflow, for their wickedness is great
> (Joel 3:12-13).

And another angel came out of the temple which is in heaven, and he also had a sharp sickle. And another angel, the one who has power over fire, came out from the altar; and he called with a loud voice to him who had the sharp sickle, saying, "Put in your sharp sickle, and gather the clusters from the vine of the earth, because her grapes are ripe." And the angel swung his sickle to the earth, and gathered the clusters from the vine of the earth, and threw them into the great wine press of the wrath of God. And the wine press was trodden outside the city, and blood came out from the wine press, up to the horses' bridles, for a distance of two hundred miles (Rev. 14:17-20).

The world, and most of Christianity, thinks of Armageddon as a huge, raging battle between the forces of good and evil. Many will indeed be slaughtered there, but it will be the most lopsided battle ever; it is Satan's armies that shall shed every drop of blood. The symbolism of the sword out of the mouth of Jesus shows that He does not have to swing an actual sword or bloody Himself in combat (Rev. 19:15-16). He will speak the word, and it will be carried out.

THE ANTICHRIST AND FALSE PROPHET
TO THE FIERY LAKE

The majority of people reading this know that the words of the Bible are settled, as if they are already accomplished. Daniel was told that the Antichrist will try to change laws (both God's laws and things prophesied) and times (when God has ordained that they will take place) (Dan. 7:25). He keeps trying, even while watching all prophecy come to pass exactly as described in God's Word. The battle of Armageddon will be the final defeat of the Antichrist and the False Prophet, and their end will be added to the list of prophecies literally fulfilled.

And the beast was seized, and with him the false prophet who performed the signs in his presence, by which he deceived those who had received the mark of the beast and those who worshiped his image; these two were thrown alive into the lake of fire which burns with brimstone (Rev. 19:20).

SATAN CONFINED IN THE ABYSS

And I saw an angel coming down from heaven, having the key of the abyss and a great chain in his hand. And he laid hold of the dragon, the serpent of old, who is the devil and Satan, and bound him for a thousand years, and threw him into the abyss, and shut it and sealed it over him, so that he should not deceive the nations any longer, until the thousand years were completed; after these things he must be released for a short time (Rev. 20:1-3).

One could ask why Satan will be detained in the pit, while the Antichrist and False Prophet are thrown into an eternal lake of fire, and why he will be released at the end of the thousand years. The answer may be found in the nature of a just God (in a legal sense). On the human level, one might question whether persons living in the present age, having the presence of Satan to tempt them, should be judged the same way that another living in the near-perfect environment of the Kingdom would be judged. By allowing Satan to test the mortals who live in the Kingdom, each must make his or her own moral decision for good or evil. After that, Satan will also be confined to the punishment of the fiery lake.

The Sheep and Goat Judgment

The restoration of the earth in preparation for the Kingdom includes the selection of people that will inhabit the kingdom period. The Gentiles who will enter the kingdom are determined in the judgment of the Sheep and the Goats nations. This judgment is not found explicitly in the Old Testament, except perhaps in Psalm 21:9 and Zephaniah 3:8-9, but it figures prominently in the Olivet discourse.

Amazingly, there will be some who survive the ordeals of the Tribulation, the Wrath, and the Battle of Armageddon. Even though the influence of the Antichrist will be felt all over the earth, there will be a large number of Gentiles who will not worship him or take his mark. These Gentiles will be judged to determine that they are worthy to enter the Kingdom, with the selection criteria based upon how they treated the elect during the Tribulation. This is not a courtroom trial, because there is no debate, no jury, and no appeal of the verdict. Judgment is to be pronounced upon the testimony of only one person, the Lord Jesus Christ.

> But when the Son of Man comes in His glory, and all the angels with Him, then He will sit on His glorious throne. And all the nations [gentiles] will be gathered before Him; and He will separate them from one another, as the shepherd separates the sheep from the goats; and He will put the sheep on His right, and the goats on the left. Then the King will say to those on His right, "Come, you who are blessed of My Father, inherit the kingdom prepared for you from the foundation of the world For I was hungry, and you gave Me something to eat; I was thirsty, and you gave Me drink; I was a stranger, and you invited Me in; naked, and you clothed Me; I was sick, and you visited Me; I was in prison, and you came to Me....Truly I say to you, to the extent that you

did it to one of these brothers of Mine, even the least of them, you did it to Me."

Then He will also say to those on His left, "Depart from Me, accursed ones, into the eternal fire which has been prepared for the devil and his angels....truly I say to you, to the extent that you did not do it to one of the least of these, you did not do it to Me." And these will go away into eternal punishment, but the righteous into eternal life (Matt. 25:31-46 [some omissions for brevity]).

This Scripture demonstrates the extent of the mercy of God and His righteousness. Those who enter the kingdom will have assisted the saints and Jews when they could not buy or sell, had their homes seized, and were imprisoned during the Tribulation. They will not have "accepted the Lord Jesus" as we would say, but did themselves show mercy to those who had. They are declared "righteous" and allowed to enter the kingdom. Emphatically, this is not a picture of the church, because it is a judgment based solely of works, not of faith.

The "goats," or the wicked in this judgment, are taken out to be burned in the last event of the Day of the Lord, the Renovation of the earth by fire. The significant difference between this judgment and the Rapture is that the wicked are removed and the righteous left in this parable. In the Rapture, the righteous are taken out of the earth and the wicked are left.

RE-GATHERING OF THE JEWS TO ISRAEL

The world Jewish population today is about sixteen million people. Of this number, just fewer than six million live in the United States and five and one-half million live in Israel;[22] with the rest primarily in Europe. The Bible says that those who survive "The Time of Jacob's Trouble" will be gathered back to Israel in the end times, that is, the Day of the Lord, with *none* left in captivity (Ezek. 39:28). How will such a tremendous ingathering take place?

We are not talking about the relative few who are now immigrating to Israel on a fairly regular basis. It will exceed the Exodus in its scope and importance.

> "Therefore behold, days are coming," declares the Lord, "when it will no longer be said, 'As the Lord lives, who brought up the sons of Israel out of the land of Egypt,' but, 'As the Lord lives, who brought up the sons of Israel from the land of the north and from all the countries where He had banished them.' For I will restore them to their own land which I gave to their fathers" (Jer. 16:14-15).

While many Jews may be returning to Israel for altruistic reasons, in the last days their purpose will be to flee persecution. Hosea said that, in the end-time, they would seek God "in their affliction" (Hosea 5:15), bringing to mind the coming "time of Jacob's trouble" in the last days when they will "be hated of all nations" (Matt. 24:9). The time of intense persecution will begin with the Abomination.

They will be gathered from "the four corners of the earth" (Isa. 11:12) with "an outstretched arm and with wrath poured out" (Ezek. 20:34). The diligence with which God will seek them out is seen in these passages:

> Behold, I am going to send for many fishermen," declares the Lord, "and they will fish for them; and afterwards I shall send for many hunters, and they will hunt them from every mountain and every hill, and from the clefts of the rocks. For My eyes are on all their ways; they are not hidden from My face, nor is their iniquity concealed from My eyes (Jer. 16:16-17).

> For thus says the Lord, "Sing aloud with gladness for Jacob, and shout among the chiefs of the nations; proclaim, give praise, and say, 'O Lord, save Thy people, the remnant of Israel.' Behold, I am bringing them from the north country, and I will gather them from the remote parts of the earth, among them the blind and the lame, the woman with child and she who is in labor with child, together; a great company, they shall return here" (Jer. 31:7-8).

He will bring them all out to a place where He will judge them face to face, and destroy those who love detestable things (Ezek. 20:33-38). Only one-third of the Jews in that day will actually enter the Kingdom (Zech. 13:8-9), but those that do will bring the wealth of the nations with them (Isa. 60:9-11; Zech. 2:9; 14:14).

PURIFICATION OF THE EARTH WITH FIRE

The second woe of the trumpet judgments will leave as many as two billion, but at least 500 million dead and presumably lying exposed on the ground.[23] The Wrath of God, as expressed in the bowl judgments, inflicts severe injury to the earth and death to many of the remaining inhabitants on land and sea. God is going to purge His people of those who are unworthy, as we just discussed. When Christ returns to earth with His armies, His first task will be the destruction of the armies that have assembled at Megiddo and Jerusalem, another 200 million.

The fires of renovation will be necessary to clean up this mess. The earth must be purged of all evil in preparation for the Kingdom that Christ will rule. It is described as total consumption of the earth, and yet it will not only leave righteous people unharmed, but they will be healed of any infirmary, so as to be fit for service in the Kingdom (See the Malachi reference below).

> But the present heavens and earth by His word are being reserved for fire, kept for the day of judgment and destruction of ungodly men (2 Pet. 3:7).

> But the day of the Lord will come like a thief, in which the heavens will pass away with a roar and the elements will be destroyed with intense heat, and the earth and its works will be burned up. Since all these things are to be destroyed in this way, what sort of people ought you to be in holy conduct and godliness, looking for and hastening the coming of the day of God, on account of which the heavens will be destroyed by burning, and the elements will melt with intense heat! But according to His promise we are

looking for new heavens and a new earth, in which righteousness dwells (2 Pet. 3:10-13).

> The Mighty One, God, the Lord, has spoken,
> And summoned the earth from the rising of the sun to its setting.
> Out of Zion, the perfection of beauty, God has shone forth.
> May our God come and not keep silence;
> Fire devours before Him,
> And it is very tempestuous around Him.
> He summons the heavens above,
> And the earth, to judge His people:
> Gather My godly ones to Me,
> Those who have made a covenant with Me by sacrifice"
> (Ps. 50:1-5).

The difficulty with understanding the fiery renovation of the earth is that there are things that one would expect to be consumed, but are not. Some who cannot accept this as a literal interpretation say that it is allegorical and that we have to find a spiritual message in these passages. To help us accept the literal interpretation, we have only to remember a similar event in the book of Daniel, when the three men were thrown into a super-heated furnace and walked around in the fire as if it were a summer stroll, while the servants of the king were killed by the heat at the mouth of the furnace. By faith we have to believe the Bible:

> You have conceived chaff, you will give birth to stubble;
> My breath will consume you like a fire. and the peoples will be burned to lime, like cut thorns which are burned in the fire. You who are far away, hear what I have done; and you who are near, acknowledge My might.
> Sinners in Zion are terrified; trembling has seized the godless. Who among us can live with the consuming fire? Who among us can live with continual burning?
> He who walks righteously, and speaks with sincerity,
> He who rejects unjust gain, and shakes his hands so that they hold no bribe;

He who stops his ears from hearing about bloodshed, and shuts his eyes from looking upon evil; (Isa. 33:11-15).

"For behold, the day is coming, burning like a furnace; and all the arrogant and every evildoer will be chaff; and the day that is coming will set them ablaze," says the Lord of hosts, "so that it will leave them neither root nor branch. But for you who fear My name the sun of righteousness will rise with healing in its wings; and you will go forth and skip about like calves from the stall. And you will tread down the wicked, for they shall be ashes under the soles of your feet on the day which I am preparing," says the Lord of hosts (Mal. 4:1-3).

Now this is a wonderful and incomprehensible thing! This "sun of righteousness," will reduce the evil person and the old creation to cinders, while at the very same time, heal the righteous. I can't explain it; I just praise God for its provision.

Think of it. All remnants of evil will be erased from the earth. No one entering the Kingdom will have any disease. No wicked will be left on the earth. A child will not happen upon some hidden pornography. No film, tapes, hard drives, or DVD's depicting violence or any sin or evil will survive the flames. No book or magazine containing blasphemy will be found. Homes and personal possessions will be safe from pilfering or vandalism. No one will assault you at home or in the streets. The elements of war will be gone. Drugs and drug paraphernalia will not be in evidence. There will be no discrimination or patronization, either political or commercial, to favor one group over another. The air will be free of any pollution.

Although it doesn't say so, it would appear that the army of the Lord might be the instrument that performs the cleansing and the selection.

Blow a trumpet in Zion, and sound an alarm on My holy mountain! Let all the inhabitants of the land tremble, for the day of the Lord is coming; surely it is near, a day of darkness and gloom, a day of clouds and thick darkness.

As the dawn is spread over the mountains, so there is a great and mighty people; there has never been anything like it, nor will there be again after it to the years of many generations.

A fire consumes before them, and behind them a flame burns. The land is like the garden of Eden before them, but a desolate wilderness behind them, and nothing at all escapes them. Their appearance is like the appearance of horses; and like war horses, so they run. With a noise as of chariots They leap on the tops of the mountains, like the crackling of a flame of fire consuming the stubble, like a mighty people arranged for battle. Before them the people are in anguish; all faces turn pale. They run like mighty men; they climb the wall like soldiers; and they each march in line, nor do they deviate from their paths. They do not crowd each other; they march everyone in his path. When they burst through the defenses, they do not break ranks. They rush on the city, they run on the wall; they climb into the houses, they enter through the windows like a thief. Before them the earth quakes, the heavens tremble, the sun and the moon grow dark, and the stars lose their brightness.

And the Lord utters His voice before His army; surely His camp is very great, for strong is he who carries out His word. The day of the Lord is indeed great and very awesome, and who can endure it? (Joel 2:1-11).

THE BATTLE OF GOG AND MAGOG

The current turmoil in the Middle East has generated a renewal of deep interest in, and much commentary about the "Battle of Gog and Magog," described in Ezekiel chapters 38 and 39. Magog is described as a country to the far north of Israel, and the other enemies of Israel listed as participants in this battle are currently Muslim countries. There is no consensus of the time of this battle, which most believe will be fought at some time in the seventieth week of Daniel.

We are convinced that this battle will not happen within the scope of the seventy weeks of Daniel. The Revelation places it, or a similar battle, at the end of the Millennium, when Satan will be loosed from his thousand-year confinement in the abyss.

> And when the thousand years are completed, Satan will be released from his prison, and will come out to deceive the nations which are in the four corners of the earth, Gog and Magog, to gather them together for the war; the number of them is like the sand of the seashore. And they came up on the broad plain of the earth and surrounded the camp of the saints and the beloved city, and fire came down from heaven and devoured them (Rev. 20:7-9).

Following are the reasons the battle will take place a thousand years later than many say it will:

1. The weapons described are all primitive by twenty-first century standards, but they would be appropriate at the end of the Millennium, during which modern weapons of warfare will have been destroyed and men will "study war no more" (Isa. 2:4). An uprising against Israel at this time would probably not be waged with modern weapons, but they could use implements like swords, bows and arrows, spears, shields, etc.

    We understand that the ancient prophets, if seeing modern warfare in visions, would not have the vocabulary to describe rifles, mortars, tanks, etc. and we cannot conclude from language alone what weaponry would be used.
2. The battle will take place after the Jews have returned to their land, and "living securely, all of them" (Eze. 38:8). The premise of chapter seven of this book is that this comes with the Millennium.
3. The land will have been "restored from the sword," which does not describe Israel before the Millennium (Eze. 38:8).
4. Israel is described as "a land of unwalled villages," "living without walls, and having no bars or gates" (Eze. 38:11). In Ezekiel's day, the walls of a city describes one that has protection. An unwalled city was one without defenses. That is not true of Israel today; it will be true in the Millennium.

5. The people will have had time to accumulate cattle and wealth and will be living in the "navel" (center) of the world (Eze. 38:12).

6. Both passages prophesy that God will rain down fire upon Gog, his troops, and all who are with him (Eze. 38:22 and Rev. 20:9).

7. It will take seven months to bury the enemy dead to cleanse the land (Eze. 39:12). This is not the cleansing of the entire earth by fire in the Day of the Lord, which must be done in the last forty-five days of the end of this age in preparation of the Millennium.

CLOSING COMMENTS

At the outset of this chapter, we said that no one has to subject himself to the horrors of the Day of the Lord. It should be evident by now that the one who has put his hope for salvation and eternal life in Christ Jesus will have been removed from the earth in the Day of Christ before the Day of the Lord, and thus, will not be present to see and experience the Wrath of God.

If you have not placed your faith in the provision that God has made for your "great escape," you can do it at this very moment. Talk to God right where you are, and tell Him of your decision to place your trust in His Son, Jesus. He has promised that the Holy Spirit will enter you and instruct you further. Don't delay; do it now.

The Day of the Lord is closed when King Jesus takes possession of the purged and renovated earth in a period of time we call "The Millennium." Only those mortal humans who have been declared righteous will enter the kingdom for a thousand years. Those who were saved before the Resurrection and Rapture, including you, if you just made the commitment we just invited you to do, will be with Jesus in their spiritual bodies.

4

The Olivet Discourse

Groups of Faithful pilgrims were making their way up the road to Jerusalem, chatting about their long journeys and the Passover celebration they would observe in a few days. Some of the pilgrims noticed Jesus with His disciples and excitedly pointed Him out to their friends, telling them how He had been healing the sick on this journey, and that He had even raised a man named Lazarus from the dead a short while ago! As the talk spread, a growing crowd began to proclaim Him as the Messiah, laying their coats and palm fronds in front of the donkey He was riding. Today we celebrate that occasion as "Palm Sunday."

Jesus and the disciples went into the temple and looked around before walking back to Bethany to stay with Lazarus and His sisters, Mary and Martha. They returned to the temple the next day, and perhaps because He knew that His days on earth were few, Jesus became so incensed at those who were commercializing the offering of temple sacrifices that He angrily overturned their tables and drove their animals out of the courtyard. By Mark's account, He encountered the religious leaders that day and the next. The chief priests and the scribes saw that their authority was being challenged and decided that He must be killed.

The discussion with the disciples we are going to explore took place Tuesday evening on the Mount of Olives in full view of the Temple Mount. Matthew wrote that "the disciples" came to Jesus privately; Luke reads "some disciples," and Mark tells us that they were Peter, James, John, and Andrew. On this hilltop, Jesus delivered "The Olivet discourse," recorded in Matthew 24 and 25, Mark 13, Luke 17:20-37 and

Luke 21. These were Jesus' last words regarding the end of the age before He was put to death.

On Thursday evening, they observed the Passover supper, and the following day, Jesus was crucified.

In previous chapters, we considered end-time events in their general chronological order, based upon the prophecy delivered to Daniel regarding the future of Israel, expressed in terms of seventy "weeks" of years. Now we want to consider Matthew's account of Jesus' commentary on the seventieth week. As you read His words, keep in mind that He was having a conversation with Jewish men in spiritual transition, men who were raised in the culture of the old covenant, but to whom He had been teaching the kingdom of Heaven for the last three years. They knew little or nothing about the coming church.

This is not to say that the Olivet discourse is meant only for Jews, although only Jews were present. He also intended it for the church of the latter days, because He also said, "You will be hated on account of my name." As we pointed out before, Christians must also take the warnings and admonitions to heart, because Satan will persecute all who worship the one true God (Rev. 12:17).

The Bible record presents Jesus' comments as a monologue, but it is likely a compilation of Jesus' answers to questions the disciples asked Him in a protracted discussion of the end of the age. For the convenience of this study, we partition it to reflect the different directions the conversation took in the course of the evening.

THE SETTING FOR THE DISCOURSE

You have probably seen one of the popular panoramic pictures of the Temple Mount taken from the Mount of Olives. This is the best place to replicate what Jesus and His disciples were looking at that evening, except that a magnificent alabaster and gold temple complex sat where the golden domed mosque is today.

We are told that when Jesus visited Jerusalem, He often went to the Olive groves on that hill to meditate and pray. He would have left the temple mount through a gate in the huge stone wall, walked down into

the Kidron Valley and up the slopes of the Mount of Olives. His disciples may have paused on the ascent to look backwards at the temple.
They hadn't been to the city that often, and when they did, they saw significant progress in the temple construction.

> And Jesus came out from the temple and was going away when
> His disciples came up to point out the temple buildings to Him.
> And He answered and said to them, "Do you not see all these
> things? Truly I say to you, not one stone here shall be left upon
> another, which will not be torn down."
> And as He was sitting on the Mount of Olives, the disciples
> came to Him privately, saying, "Tell us, when will these things
> be, and what will be the sign of Your coming, and of the end
> of the age?" (Matt. 24:1-3).

As they continued up the slopes of the Mount of Olives, they had
time to reflect on what He had just told them. When they were settling
for the night, they finally asked *when* these things would take place, and
what *sign* they could associate with the Lord's return at the end of the age.

The Jewish Temples

Since the temples that were built and destroyed in Jerusalem figure
prominently in Jewish history and prophecy, a few words about them
may be helpful to our understanding of the text. In the years before
967 BC, King Solomon built an ornate temple, which was the center
of their culture for years, even after they began to worship idols and
the Spirit of God departed the building. In 586 BC, about twenty
years into the seventy-year Exile, it was destroyed by the Babylonians,
to lie in ruins for the remainder of the Captivity. It was rebuilt after
the Exile, but it did not approach the beauty of the original.
Nevertheless, it was very important that the prescribed sacrificial offerings were again being observed. Much later, about fourteen years
before Jesus was born, King Herod began to enlarge and beautify the
temple complex by adding new buildings and putting an alabaster and

gold façade on the structures in a plan to win the favor of the Jews while creating a legacy for himself.

JESUS' OVERVIEW OF THE END TIMES

Jesus' answer to their question about the *time* and the *sign* was a brief overview of the end time, from the beginning of birth pains to the end of the age:

> And Jesus answered and said to them, "See to it that no one misleads you. For many will come in My name, saying, 'I am the Christ,' and will mislead many. And you will be hearing of wars and rumors of wars; see that you are not frightened, for those things must take place, but that is not yet the end. For nation will rise against nation, and kingdom against kingdom, and in various places there will be famines and earthquakes. But all these things are merely the beginning of birth pangs.
>
> "Then they will deliver you to tribulation, and will kill you, and you will be hated by all nations on account of My name. And at that time many will fall away and will deliver up one another and hate one another. And many false prophets will arise, and will mislead many. And because lawlessness is increased, most people's love will grow cold. But the one who endures to the end, he shall be saved. And this gospel of the kingdom shall be preached in the whole world for a witness to all the nations, and then the end shall come" (Matt. 24:4-14).

The references to tribulation and the Abomination in the next verse (verse 15) leave no doubt that Jesus was commenting on the seventieth week of Daniel that will conclude the age in which we are living.

The First Half of the Week, the Beginning of Birth Pains

In His response, Jesus first told them what the sign of the end of the age would *not* be. He gave them a list of things that would take place, but added that they should *not* be taken as indicative of the immediate end of the age. That list included:

- Many calling themselves "Christ."
- Wars and rumors of wars, by kingdoms and nations.
- Famines in many places, followed by many deaths.
- Earthquakes in diverse places.

You must resist the temptation to cite the very things that Jesus said were *not* signs of the end times to prove that we *are* in the end times, for example, after a major earthquake or natural disaster. The reason they cannot be the definitive sign of the end, is that wars, famines, and earthquakes have been with us continually since the beginning of the human race, and are therefore uncertain predictors of the arrival of this most significant period of eschatology.

The earthquakes, famines, and wars that are coming in the seventieth week will be of unusual frequency and intensity compared with those we have experienced. Some say that the number of strong earthquakes in recent years is significantly above average, but the U.S. government agency responsible for tracking such things have data that show that earthquake activity is no more intense now than it has been since we began measuring them.[24] Yes, we hear more about earthquakes that we have in years past, for two good reasons. First, we live in an age of expanding communication, and when something happens in the most remote parts of earth, we know of it almost instantaneously. Second, there were only 350 earthquake monitoring stations in 1931, but in 2006, there are over 4,000 very sensitive seismographs installed all over the world with the ability to detect thousands of earth tremors that we cannot feel even if we are sitting above them.[25]

I also have to say that in my lifetime, the world has not seen the terrible famines and plagues of past years, thanks in part to medical advances and the ability to transport food and medicines quickly to all parts of the globe. Our greatest fears regarding plagues are that man will develop microorganisms that are resistant to the cures we develop to combat them, or that a mutant strain will suddenly surface that we are unable to constrain, or that some terrorist group will use them in weapons of mass destruction. The Bible says that they are coming. It is certain (Rev. 6:8).

The Bible student living in that last generation will recognize these things for what they are. Those insightful few may also identify the covenant that initiates the last week, but there will be one sign in the middle of the week that only the spiritually blind could miss.

The things that constitute the "beginning of birth pains" are very similar to the things John saw when the first four seals were broken (Rev. 6:1-8). We will elaborate upon that in the next chapter.

INTRODUCTION TO THE SECOND
HALF OF THE WEEK

When Jesus said that the elect would be delivered up to tribulation, He was telling them what was coming after the Abomination in the middle of Daniel's last week. He listed the stresses that await the righteous when the Antichrist is revealed in the middle of the week and we enter into the Tribulation (Matt. 24:9-14).

- Persecution
- Death
- Betrayal by family
- Hated of all Nations because of Jesus
- Apostasy
- False prophets deceiving many
- Increased wickedness and love growing cold
- The Saint that stands firm (overcomes) will be saved (physically)
- The gospel will be preached to the entire world

There is an old maxim about human nature, "When the going gets tough, the tough get going." Sometimes it takes a difficult situation to bring out the better qualities in people. In the Tribulation, Jews and Christians will stand up for God in a way they do not when things are going well. Many Jews will recognize the Lord Jesus Christ as Messiah (Zech.13:9), but there will also be professing believers who will cave under pressure and become the apostates that Paul wrote about (2 Thess. 2:3). While the more diligent Jews and Christians will be sealed for their protection from these things (Rev. 3:10; 7:3), others will be martyred for their faith (Rev. 7:14).

Despite persecution, the gospel of the Kingdom will be preached to the entire world in those times of distress. Some have taken this to be a mandate that the church or the 144,000 sanctified Jews must fulfill before the end will come, but this is absolutely not so! We should be trying to reach the world by every means available to us because we are commanded to do it, but the ultimate fulfillment of this promise is found in the Revelation:

> I saw another angel flying in midheaven, having an eternal gospel to preach to those who live on the earth, and to every nation and tribe and tongue and people (Rev. 14:6).

There is no indication that there will be any human response to the angelic preaching of this word, but after this, there will be no living person who will be able to say that they had not heard the gospel from an authoritative source.

THE TRIBULATION

Jesus had just told the disciples that they would be delivered up to tribulation, betrayal, and death. Now they, like you and I, had we been told this, wanted to know what they should do in these circumstances and when, before the end, they would be rescued (as Daniel put it). Jesus' answer is:

> "Therefore when you see the abomination of desolation which was spoken of through Daniel the prophet, standing in the holy place (let the reader understand), then let those who are in Judea flee to the mountains; let him who is on the housetop not go

down to get the things out that are in his house; and let him who
is in the field not turn back to get his cloak. But woe to those who
are with child and to those who nurse babes in those days! But
pray that your flight may not be in the winter, or on a Sabbath;
for then there will be a great tribulation, such as has not occurred
since the beginning of the world until now, nor ever shall. And
unless those days had been cut short, no life would have been
saved; but for the sake of the elect those days shall be cut short.
Then if anyone says to you, 'Behold, here is the Christ,' or 'There
He is,' do not believe him. For false Christs and false prophets
will arise and will show great signs and wonders, so as to mislead,
if possible, even the elect. Behold, I have told you in advance. If
therefore they say to you, 'Behold, He is in the wilderness,' do not
go forth, or, 'Behold, He is in the inner rooms,' do not believe
them. For just as the lightning comes from the east, and flashes
even to the west, so shall the coming of the Son of Man be.
Wherever the corpse is, there the vultures will gather" (Matt.
24:15-28).

Having given His overview of the future of Israel through the end of
the age, Jesus returns to the subject of the tribulation that will come after
the middle of the week, now calling it "The Great Tribulation." He tells
the disciples that the sign that the end of the age is near will be the abomination of desolation. He said, "When you SEE the Abomination..."
you must immediately flee to the wilderness. The purpose of any sign is
to be an unambiguous early warning so that those who see it can respond
appropriately, whether it is on the highway, in a weather forecast, or the
announced fulfillment of prophecy.

Their flight into hiding is described allegorically in Revelation 12:6,
"And the woman [Israel] fled into the wilderness where she had a place
prepared by God, so that there she might be nourished for one thousand
two hundred and sixty days." Keep in mind that Jesus was talking to Jews
in Judea about a thing that Jeremiah called "The time of Jacob's trouble."
The warning, perhaps not carrying the same degree of urgency, should
be taken to heart by Jews and Christians in every country of the world.

The Abomination initiates a period of tribulation so intense that nothing like it would be seen either before or after it (see also Daniel 12:1). The things that affect the life of the Believer before the Abomination may be stressful, but they are nothing compared to those that will follow in the Tribulation.

The Tribulation has been decreed to continue for 1,260 days (Dan. 7:25; 12:7; Rev. 12:6, 14; Revelation 13:5), but no longer than that because, "Unless those days had been cut short, no life would have been saved; but for the sake of the elect those days shall be cut short" (Matt. 24:22; Mark 13:20). The Trumpet Judgments of the Revelation reflect the terrible events of that period, and the two witnesses are the only tangible opposition to the Antichrist during that time. The Rapture ends the Tribulation of the saints, but it does not end the seventieth week or the Time of Jacob's trouble, because the Day of the Lord immediately follows.

With a large number of God's people having heeded the sign and having disappeared into "the wilderness," the Antichrist will do anything he can to trick them into coming out of hiding. Specifically, he will send false prophets to perform miracles similar to the ones the two witnesses demonstrate (Rev. 11:5-6; 13:14). Jesus warns the Believer that they should not listen to reports of Christ wanting to meet them in secret places (Matt. 24:23-26). Any who fall for the deceit and show up to meet the Messiah will be killed. Euphemistically speaking, they will be "vulture food."

When the true Christ comes, He will not be found in some announced location, waiting for people to RSVP ("Here is the Christ" in a secret room, or "There He is" in a wilderness location). The actual coming of the Son of Man will be in the clouds, unexpected, quick, and specifically from east to west (verse 27). Anyone familiar with thunderstorms knows that lightning has no directional preference, so to what does this refer? At the end of the Tribulation, the Lord and the heavenly host will appear over Jerusalem to receive the two witnesses (and all of the dead in Christ) with a shout, and to summon the elect in the Rapture with the trumpet sound (Rev. 11:15-18). The "east to west" reference reminds us that the sun appears to travel east to west due to the earth's

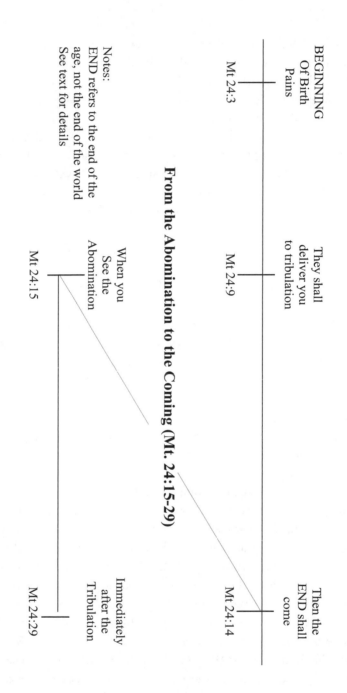

Figure 4-1, Organization of the Olivet Discourse

rotation. Could it be that the heavenly hosts remain stationary in the atmosphere while the earth with the saints pass beneath them, or will Christ and the angels sweep around the globe to gather the church while the enemies of Christ look on with awe and mourning?

"But," you ask, "won't the Rapture take place in an instant (1 Cor. 15:51-52)?" That has been taught and repeated often, but the brief answer is "probably not." In those verses, Paul was discussing the exchange of our mortal bodies for incorruptible bodies, and says that we will all be changed or *translated* in the twinkling of an eye, not that we will be caught up to meet Jesus in an instant.

Recall that when Jesus was raised from the dead, tombs were opened and the dead appeared to many as a witness of the Resurrection (Matt. 27:52-53). It would be appropriate that the person and works of the Son of God be magnified before the heathen, as hundreds of millions of saints around the world are transformed in their spiritual bodies and witness to the wicked who had worked hard to remove any mention of the Lord Jesus Christ from public display or mention. It is only right that they should see the saints received in the clouds, with adequate time to mourn the salvation they have rejected and hide themselves in the rocks and caves in an attempt to escape the wrath to come.

THE COMING OF CHRIST

There are clearly two components to the return of Christ to the earth. One we call "The Rapture," and the other we call "The Second Coming." The Rapture describes the time that Jesus will appear in the clouds with His angels to resurrect the dead in Christ and to call the living of His church from the earth. The Second Coming is so-called because He will return to the earth the same way He left it, that is, He will descend from the clouds to the Mount of Olives (Acts 1:9-11, Zech. 14:4). The pretribulation theory separates the two events by seven years, while the classic post-tribulationist says that they are one swift event.

Have you noticed that the Bible speaks of only one "coming" (parousia) of Jesus? This Greek word and the word from which it derives are the only ones used for the coming of Christ, but there is nothing sacred about it; they are also used in secular applications. Most of the times, the context makes it clear that the coming is the Rapture, but at least twice, it is the Second Coming that is being described. The Rapture and the Second Coming are two parts of one event, implying that one follows the other without much intervening time.

We will see in the Revelation that the Rapture happens at the seventh trumpet, and that the Second Coming comes after the seventh bowl. There are things to be accomplished on earth between the two events, specifically, the Wrath of God poured out on the wicked as described in the Bowl Judgments, and the destruction of spiritual Babylon. The time between the two phases of His coming is a mere thirty days. This is truly the Day of the Lord.

Jesus clearly told us the time of the Rapture relative to the Tribulation when He said:

> But <u>immediately after the tribulation</u> of those days the sun will be darkened, and the moon will not give its light, and the stars will fall from the sky, and the powers of the heavens will be shaken, and then the sign of the Son of Man will appear in the sky, and then all the tribes of the earth will mourn, and they will see the Son of Man coming on the clouds of the sky with power and great glory. And He will send forth His angels with a great trumpet and they will gather together His elect from the four winds, from one end of the sky to the other (Matt. 24:29-31 [See also Mark 13:24-27; Luke 21:25-28; and Rev. 11:15-19]).

Having warned the disciples of persecution to follow the Abomination, Jesus said that He would come in the clouds with a multitude of angels right after that, for the purpose of gathering His elect. The same celestial signs that draw attention to this event are also those that characterize the beginning of the Day of the Lord, which leads us to believe that the Resurrection and Rapture (the Day of Christ) are either the first events of the Day of the Lord, or the last things that precede it.

A correct interpretation of the Bible will be complemented by other

Scriptures. There are at least six things in this account that agree with Paul's description of the Rapture.

1) The appearing of Christ in the clouds. "…a cloud received Him out of their sight." (Acts 1:9-11); "we who are still alive and are left will be caught up together with them in the clouds to meet the Lord in the air." (1 Thess. 4:17).

2) The presence of holy angels. "…with the voice of the archangel…" (1 Thess. 4:16).

3) The gathering of the elect in the air. "…to meet the Lord in the air" (1 Thess. 4:17).

Mark and Luke (see below) differ slightly in their description of the gathering of the elect. Luke says that, "redemption is drawing near." Mark wrote that, "He will send his angels and gather his elect from the four winds, from the ends of the earth, to the ends of the heavens."

4, 5) Two groups of people are involved, the dead in Christ and the living Saints. "For if we believe that Jesus died and rose again, even so God will bring with Him those who have fallen asleep in Jesus. Then we who are alive and remain shall be caught up together with them in the clouds to meet the Lord in the air, and thus we shall always be with the Lord…" (1 Thess. 4:14,17).

6) The sound of a trumpet. "…and with the trumpet call of Go…" (1 Thess. 4:16); "…at the last trumpet…" (1 Cor. 15:52).

FURTHER SIGNS OF THE END TIMES

Jesus has just given the disciples a lot to think about. In Judea, they are to flee to the wilderness when they see the abomination, and how Satan will try to trick them into coming out of hiding. He described His return to take them out of the Tribulation, with celestial signs of the Day of the Lord and the gathering of the saints accompanied by a shout of the angel. The next part of the discourse suggests that they asked how everyday life would change before His return, or what it would be like in other parts of the world that would indicate that it was near.

The Fig Tree

Now learn the parable from the fig tree: when its branch has already become tender, and puts forth its leaves, you know that summer is near; even so you too, when you see all these things, recognize that He is near, right at the door. Truly I say to you, this generation will not pass away until all these things take place. Heaven and earth will pass away, but My words shall not pass away (Matt. 24:32-35).

He said (author's paraphrase), "Look, you know that when you see buds on the fig tree ['and ALL the trees' (Luke 21:29)], summer is coming soon. Likewise, when you see the things I have just told you about beginning to take place, be assured that every single one of them must be literally fulfilled before the end." This is a very powerful statement regarding the precision of prophecy, and only the second time He said this.

These words were spoken to the disciples, but they were intended for the last generation of this present age, since obviously the disciples never saw "all these things," and neither has anyone else up to the present time. The time is soon coming when they will begin to unfold before our eyes.

When Israel became a nation with a declaration of the United Nations in May, 1948, some began to associate that fact with the "budding of the fig tree, pointing out that the Old Testament used the fig tree to illustrate truths about Israel (Jer. 24:1-8). Some even tried to predict the time of Jesus' return by adding the years of a generation to 1948. When that didn't work too well, some repeated the process using 1967, the year that Israel took possession of the eastern part of Jerusalem and the Temple Mount.

Others point out that another translation of the word for "generation" is "race," and they say that the Jewish *race* will not pass before all these things are seen. This is a trivial interpretation, since we have a number of prophecies confirming the everlasting nature of the final Jewish kingdom.

The Time of the Coming.

The Bible tells us that the unsaved will be caught totally unawares at Jesus' coming (it will come upon them as a thief in the night) but that those who are alert and informed will know that it is near. In this discourse, there are several warning events that precede the unmistakable sign of the abomination of desolation. These include the covenant, the beginning of birth pains, and armies surrounding Jerusalem. Once they see the Abomination, they will be able to count the days until God will "rescue" them (Dan. 12:1, 7). Persistently, Daniel asked for further explanation and was told that the words would be concealed until the end time. The disciples asked Jesus a similar question about His return, and He said (I paraphrase), "Even I don't know."

> But of that day and hour no one knows, not even the angels of heaven, nor the Son, but the Father alone. For the coming of the Son of Man will be just like the days of Noah. For as in those days which were before the flood they were eating and drinking, they were marrying and giving in marriage, until the day that Noah entered the ark, and they did not understand until the flood came and took them all away; so shall the coming of the Son of Man be (Matt. 24:36-39).

Are you surprised that Jesus did not know the time of His own return to earth? In the flesh, He did not have the attributes of God, and what He knew was either gleaned from the Scriptures or supernaturally revealed to Him by the Father. You can be sure that He has that information now.

The Examples of Noah and Lot

Having made the statement that no one knows (present tense) the day and hour of His coming, Jesus said that conditions on the earth will be "just like the days of Noah." He could have painted a very bleak picture of the terrible sin that permeated the world at that time (Noah's family were the only ones declared to be righteous), but Jesus did not describe the wickedness and degeneration of the people. He said that just before the judgment of the flood, the prevailing mood will be one of normal, everyday life such as eating, drinking, planning weddings, planting for the next harvest and building for the future. And then the great flood "took them all away." Noah and his family learned when the flood would come only when they were told to go into the Ark they had been building for many years.

In Luke's account, Jesus also presented Lot as an example of prevailing conditions in the end-time. Lot's family was informed of the imminent destruction of Sodom only when the angels forcibly removed Lot, his wife, and two daughters from the city (Luke 17:28-30; Gen. 19:22). When Jesus comes, men will be working side by side and women will be doing their household chores together. Some will be taken and others left (Matt. 24:42).

Although the days will be unremarkable for the people of the world, the Jew and the Christian know that there will be a persecution of the elect for 1,260 days, after which they will be rescued. This is the dichotomy that confuses many Christians even today. Paul wrote:

> But <u>you</u>, brethren, are not in darkness, that the day should overtake <u>you</u> like a thief; for <u>you are all sons of light</u> and sons of day. <u>We</u> are not of night nor of darkness; so then let <u>us</u> not sleep as others do, but let <u>us</u> be alert and sober (1 Thess. 5:4-6).

Unfortunately, it is not at all certain that every Christian in the last days will know when the Lord is coming. Some of the saved will miss the signs and be surprised at the Rapture, as John warned the church at Sardis: "If therefore you will not wake up, I will come like a thief, and you will not know at what hour I will come upon you" (Rev. 3:3). Many Christian leaders of various convictions now say that they believe that we are in the last days. If so, then we should all be diligent to give attention to the subject of end-time prophecy to prepare the church for the days that are approaching and the return of Christ.

Having just said that only the Father knows when Jesus would return, He issues a warning for them to "Be on the alert!" or to paraphrase, "Don't let your guard down for a minute!" The illustration that follows is that of a man who believes that a burglar would come at a certain time, say, between midnight and dawn. He hires a security guard to be on duty every night during those hours. Imagine his consternation when the thief comes at dusk on a Sunday.

> Therefore be on the alert, for you do not know which day your Lord is coming. But be sure of this, that if the head of the house had known at what time of the night the thief was coming, he would have been on the alert and would not have allowed his house to be broken into. For this reason you be ready too; for the Son of Man is coming at an hour when you do not think He will (Matt. 24:42-44).

There have been more than a few teachers of prophecy who have studied the Jewish feasts and are convinced that Jesus must come at the time of the Feast of Trumpets. Zola Levitt was correct to write "…the trumpet unquestionably represents the rapture of the church," but this does not bind the Lord to come on that feast day.

It is no sin to arrive at a Scripture-based theory about the Lord's return as long as we don't take the attitude that we can ignore our responsibilities before that time comes. The true child of God will not be caught compromising with the world when the trumpet sounds.

KINGDOM PARABLES

The theological system that Jesus taught the disciples was that of the kingdom of Heaven, preached for the first time by John the Baptist.

The Kingdom is not the same as the church, which was birthed about fifty-three days after the Olivet discourse. Many fail to recognize the differences of the two, and they are often treated as one and the same. One could "enter" the Kingdom of Heaven by good works and adopting a strict code of compliance found in the Old Testament governing the relationships of man with God and man with fellow man. The position of a person in the Kingdom is not secure, as it is for the Christian in the body of Christ, as the parables illustrate. The Kingdom preceded the church and will remain on earth after the church is gone. The Kingdom is a spiritual one for now, but it will be a tangible one in the Millennium, with Jesus reigning from Jerusalem.

We often talk about "joining" the church, and while we may have our names enrolled in the records of a local body called a church, all true Christians are baptized into Christ's church by the Holy Spirit in a spiritual union with God. The Christian becomes a new person when he or she expresses faith in Jesus as the Son of God, and this is confessed before men (Rom. 10:9-10). The church is the body of Christ and no outside influence can force a division of the two.

Jesus told His followers a number of "kingdom parables," found primarily in the Olivet discourse and in Matthew 13, but they should never be used to determine church doctrine. People making up the church are citizens of the kingdom, but not all kingdom citizens are in the church. For example, we all have known really, really good people who worship God and have very high moral standards and meet every criterion that the apostle Paul spelled out for someone in the Kingdom, but who have never claimed Jesus as the only way to salvation. This will be the status of the number of Jews and Gentiles who will enter the physical kingdom in their natural bodies after having been declared righteous. The Gentiles who enter will be those "sheep nations" (see below) and the Jews will be those who are called out of nations around the world and judged before God (Ezek. 20:34-38).

The relationship of the Master and the servant in the parables that follow depends upon the servant consistently doing what he knows is right until the time that the master calls the servant into accountability.

Doing the Lord's will, the Faithful Slave and the Evil Slave
The first of the kingdom parables in the Olivet discourse contrasts the
behaviors of a good servant and an evil servant when the master is absent.

> Who then is the faithful and sensible slave whom his master put
> in charge of his household to give them their food at the proper
> time? Blessed is that slave whom his master finds so doing when
> he comes. Truly I say to you, that he will put him in charge of all
> his possessions [in the Kingdom].
>
> But if that evil slave says in his heart, 'My master is not
> coming for a long time,' and shall begin to beat his fellow
> slaves and eat and drink with drunkards; the master of that
> slave will come on a day when he does not expect him and at
> an hour which he does not know, and shall cut him in pieces
> and assign him a place with the hypocrites; weeping shall be
> there and the gnashing of teeth (Matt. 24:45-51).

The slaves in this parable are not Christians awaiting the return of
Jesus; neither is Jesus the returning master coming to gather the church.
Jesus will not use the occasion of His coming to punish any Christian
simply because he or she is not fully prepared to meet Him, and in particular, they will not be condemned to hell. As for the Christian who is
harming the body of Christ through his words or actions, he may die pre-
maturely (1 Cor. 11:30), and his works may be burned in the fires of
testing, but he enters heaven nevertheless (1 Cor. 3:13-15).

This parable speaks to the spiritual state of the individual, who will
be permitted to enter the Kingdom, and who will not.

Prepared for his coming, the Wedding guests
The next kingdom parable is the familiar story of five wise virgins and
five foolish virgins (young women) invited to attend a wedding (Matt.
25:1-13). The application of this parable (and most parables have only
one application) is in verse 13. It is the same as Matthew 24:32. "Be on
the alert then, for you do not know the day or the hour." It would be

wrong for us to extend this teaching to the church and to conclude that a Christian would be denied heaven merely because they are not completely ready when Christ appears. It is appropriate for this action to be taken against the Jew who is unwilling to acknowledge Jesus as the Messiah or the Gentile who has rejected the gospel.

Stewardship, the Parable of the Talents

The third parable is that of a man who went on an extended journey, but before he left, he entrusted his servants to invest his money (Matt. 25:14-30). The money in this parable may be representative of the law and the prophets that God entrusted to Israel. He gave different amounts to each servant, apparently proportioned according to their known levels of responsibility. The first two each doubled what they were given by the master, but the third hid his single talent in a safe, but non-productive, place. When the master returned, two servants had good returns on their investments, but the one who hid the money was thrown into outer darkness, or what we would call "hell." That is an illustration of salvation based upon works and is not a picture of the relationship between God and the church.

Salvation by Works, the Sheep and the Goats

Some hesitate to call this narration a parable, because it reads more like a prophecy regarding the rewards and punishments of people who will have experienced the Day of the Lord. A parable is a short story that illustrates a moral or spiritual truth. It is called the "Judgment of the Sheep and Goats," and we have addressed it in the chapter The Day of the Lord. Rather than reproducing it here, I suggest you read the rather lengthy account in Matthew 25:31-46.

Note that the Goats, or the wicked, are sent to the lake of fire for eternal punishment, and the righteous are left on earth to enter the Kingdom. This is diametrically opposed to the sequence of the Rapture, where the righteous are removed from the earth while the wicked and non-Christian are left to suffer the Wrath of God. The reversed order is also found in parables of the "Wheat and Tares," and of the Good and

Bad Fish caught in the dragnet, told in Matthew 13:24-30; 47-50.

The Sheep, the wheat, and the good fish are symbolic of people who will live through the Tribulation without bending to the pressures of the Antichrist or taking his mark. They are not the body of Christ, but they will have been a comfort and sustainer of the church and righteous Jew in those difficult times. They are genuinely surprised to be declared righteous and permitted to populate the kingdom of God during the Millennium. They are not "saved" and do not have eternal life. They must face the Great White Throne judgment at the end of the Millennium. The goats, the tares, and the trash fish are the wicked that will be cast into Hades, also waiting the Great White Throne judgment. These parables make fine moral statements, but they should never be used to determine church doctrine.

SUMMARY

The Olivet discourse was Jesus' last instruction to His disciples regarding the last few years of the present age, delivered in response to their request to know the "time" of the end of the age, and a "sign" that it was near. Jesus Himself invited their inquiry with His comment that the beautiful temple being constructed by King Herod would be utterly destroyed.

The Olivet discourse complements Daniel's seventieth week of prophecy. It includes a list of "birth pains" the world must endure even before the abomination of desolation is set up in the middle of the week. The Abomination will be the catalyst for the Tribulation and all the distress that those who follow God will suffer, so Jesus told them (and us) what Satan's schemes will be, and how they (and we) should respond. He told them what the world would be like before those days should come and warned them to be ever vigilant for the time He will snatch us out of it at the end of the designated period, as well as the consequences of not being prepared.

5

The Judgments of the Revelation

As the river of prophecy flows through time, it grows wider and deeper as tributaries of additional knowledge and springs of new revelations join it. The book of Revelation is the last written prophecy of the Bible, and the most detailed. We watch for more to be unveiled in the future, since we are promised that things that were "sealed" by the prophets would be revealed in the end-times.

"The Revelation of Jesus Christ" is the only book of the Bible that carries a blessing to the one who "keeps" (KJV), "heeds" (NASB), or "takes to heart" (NIV) the prophecy it contains. Jesus Himself promised the blessing at the beginning of the book (Rev. 1:1-3), and again at the end (Rev. 22:7). Please do not deny yourself this blessing.

Despite this wonderful promise, many people avoid reading the Revelation. Some read it hastily out of a sense of duty, become overwhelmed by details and symbolism, and never read it again. A few do a disservice to the book when they lift verses out of context to "prove" some point or other. Many in positions of authority avoid teaching it because they themselves do not comprehend it.

There are five series of judgments in the Revelation, the "last word" of eschatology.

- Seven letters to seven churches (2:1-3:22)
- Seven seals (6:1-8:5)

- Seven trumpets (8:6-11:19)
- Seven thunders (10:3-4)
- Seven bowls (15:1-16:21)

LETTERS TO THE SEVEN CHURCHES (REV. 2-3)

It may come as a surprise to you that we include the letters to the seven churches in a list of divine judgments. They differ from the seals, trumpets, and bowls in that those judgments are unconditional, that is, there is nothing we can do to change their outcome. The letters, however, contain warnings of punishment that may or may not be carried out, depending upon the reader's response to the admonitions they contain. Each church had unique virtues and problems that needed to be corrected to avoid God's reprimand. The characteristics of those first century churches are still found in today's churches, and the reason the letters were written in the first place was for the edification of Christendom of all time.

Churches, like people, have personalities, which is why people look for the "right" church to attend. For some, the church must adhere to certain doctrinal positions or observe a particular order and form of worship. Others look for a church that isn't too large or too small, one that has a particular ministry, or one that has imaginative architecture in an upscale community.

The character of a church may be influenced by a denomination, or by a pastor who attended a certain school and reflects the doctrinal positions of that institution. The fact that churches have different "personalities" is not necessarily bad, as long as they embrace the revealed truths of Scripture. One could make a case for the value of a diversity of churches to accommodate the needs of particular segments of a community.

Notice that the letters are each addressed to "the angel of the church at (…)." The word "angel" simply means "messenger," who is the leader that had been sent to the church that is under scrutiny. Most of the instruction of the letters is singular, so the burden of response seems to be upon the pastor. But the people who attend those churches cannot escape the responsibility for personal repentance either. Certainly we understand that only an individual can qualify as an "overcomer."

The seven letters are messages for outsiders as well, when it repeatedly makes the statement, "He who has an ear, let him hear what the Spirit says to the churches." We who have been permitted to read the letters must also respond correctly to what Jesus said to the churches in Asia Minor a long time ago. Excerpts from the letters follow, illustrating the heart of the Spirit's message to the churches:

> *Ephesus*: But I have this against you, that <u>you have left your first love</u>. Remember therefore from where you have fallen, and repent and do the deeds you did at first; or else I am coming to you, and will remove your lampstand out of its place—unless you repent (Rev. 2:4-5).

> *Smyrna*: Do not fear what you are about to suffer. Behold, <u>the devil is about to cast some of you into prison, that you may be tested</u>, and you will have tribulation ten days. Be faithful until death, and I will give you the crown of life (Rev. 2:10).

> *Pergamum*: But I have a few things against you, because <u>you have there some who hold the</u> <u>teaching of Balaam</u>, who kept teaching Balak to put a stumbling block before the sons of Israel, to eat things sacrificed to idols, and to commit acts of immorality. Thus you also have some who in the same way hold the <u>teaching of the Nicolaitans</u>. Repent therefore; or else I am coming to you quickly, and I will make war against them with the sword of My mouth (Rev. 2:14-16).

> *Thyatira*: But I have this against you, that <u>you tolerate the woman Jezebel</u>, who calls herself a prophetess, and she teaches and leads My bond-servants astray, so that they commit acts of immorality and eat things sacrificed to idols. And I gave her time to repent; and she does not want to repent of her immorality. Behold, I will cast her upon a bed of sickness, and those who commit adultery

with her into great tribulation, unless they repent of her deeds. And I will kill her children with pestilence; and all the churches will know that I am He who searches the minds and hearts; and I will give to each one of you according to your deeds. But I say to you, the rest who are in Thyatira, who do not hold this teaching, who have not known the deep things of Satan, as they call them— I place no other burden on you. Nevertheless what you have, hold fast until I come (Rev. 2:20-25).

Sardis: Wake up, and strengthen the things that remain, which were about to die; for I have not found your deeds completed in the sight of My God. Remember therefore what you have received and heard; and keep it, and repent. If therefore you will not wake up, I will come like a thief, and you will not know at what hour I will come upon you. But you have a few people in Sardis who have not soiled their garments; and they will walk with Me in white; for they are worthy (Rev. 3:2-4).

Philadelphia: I know your deeds. Behold, I have put before you an open door which no one can shut, because you have a little power, and have kept My word, and have not denied My name. Behold, I will cause those of the synagogue of Satan, who say that they are Jews, and are not, but lie— behold, I will make them to come and bow down at your feet, and to know that I have loved you. Because you have kept the word of My perseverance, I also will keep you from the hour of testing, that hour which is about to come upon the whole world, to test those who dwell upon the earth. I am coming quickly; hold fast what you have, in order that no one take your crown (Rev. 3:8-11).

Laodicea: I know your deeds, that you are neither cold nor hot; I would that you were cold or hot. So because you are lukewarm, and neither hot nor cold, I will spit you out of My mouth. Because you say, "I am rich, and have become wealthy, and have need of nothing," and you do not know that you are wretched and miserable and poor and blind and naked, I advise you to buy from Me gold refined by fire, that you may become rich, and white garments, that you may clothe yourself, and that the shame of your nakedness may not be revealed; and eye salve to anoint your eyes, that you may see. Those whom I love, I reprove and discipline; be zealous therefore, and repent. Behold, I stand at the door and knock; if anyone hears My voice and opens the door, I will come in to him, and will dine with him, and he with Me (Rev. 3:15-21).

Escaping Tribulation

Of the seven churches, the one at Philadelphia, of whom nothing negative is said, historically has received the most attention. Jesus told them, "you have kept the word of my perseverance and I will keep you from the hour of testing." Is that a promise that you can claim that for yourself?

A popular theory conceived in the nineteenth century teaches that the seven churches represent seven church "ages," from the first century until the present. Those church ages have been defined such that we are currently living in the age of the Philadelphia church, with the promise that we will be taken out of the earth before the Tribulation period begins. According to this teaching, all who have been baptized into the church body by the Holy Spirit will be rescued from tribulation regardless of how sanctified an individual's life may be, or how far he or she may be straying from the Lord.

The theory is riddled with flaws and inconsistencies, not the least of which is that it has no foundation in Scripture. The warnings and exhortations to the six churches that need correction are just as applicable to us as is the promise to the Philadelphia church. We cannot become complacent by appropriating the most positive thought we can find, while ignoring the other admonitions. "He that has ears, let him hear what the Spirit says to the churches."

If the promise to the Philadelphia church is not the rapture of all believers, then to whom does the promise of escape apply, and what is the nature of the escape? There seems to be a parallel between the Philadelphia church and the 144,000 Jewish men who will be sealed for their protection before the Tribulation (Rev. 7:3-8; 14:1-5). Both are a limited number, both are subject to stringent selection criteria, and both will be preserved in the Tribulation by the grace of God. Every Christian and Jew wants to be "kept from the hour of testing," but not every one has chosen to "persevere in the Word" or to keep themselves spiritually chaste, and many have denied Jesus' name under social pressures. The concept is as old as this instruction:

> Seek the Lord, all you humble of the earth who have carried out His ordinances; seek righteousness, seek humility. perhaps you will be hidden in the day of the Lord's anger (Zeph. 2:3).

THE THUNDER JUDGMENTS (REV. 10:3-4)

Even though the Thunder Judgments do not immediately follow the letters, we can be done with them rather quickly, simply because we don't know anything about them, other than they were revealed to John but not recorded for us (Rev. 10:3-4). Obviously, their messages were understood, because John began to write them down before he was told to stop. The purpose of the Thunder Judgments will be known to the last generation in the end times. It may be that they will be the validation of the witnesses in the last days [see Daniel 12:9].

INTRODUCTION TO THE SEALS, TRUMPETS, AND BOWLS

Most commentators devote more of their time on the judgments of the seals, trumpets, and bowls, and that is what we shall do for the rest of this chapter. It is obvious that these three judgments are closely linked, since each of them ends with a particular phrase:

> After the seventh seal: And the angel took the censer; and he filled it with the fire of the altar and threw it to the earth; and there followed peals of thunder and sounds and flashes of lightning and an earthquake (Rev. 8:5).

After the seventh trumpet: And the temple of God which is in
heaven was opened; and the ark of His covenant appeared in His
temple, and there were <u>flashes of lightning and sounds and peals
of thunder and an earthquake and a great hailstorm</u> (Rev. 11:19)

After the seventh bowl: And there were flashes of lightning and
sounds and peals of thunder; and there was a great earthquake,
such as there had not been since man came to be upon the earth,
so great an earthquake was it, and so mighty (Rev. 16:18).

If these sights and sounds seem familiar, you may recall that we were
first introduced to them in John's description of the things he saw and
heard at God's throne in heaven. They come after each series of the judgments like a resounding "Amen!" from heaven.

And from the throne proceed <u>flashes of lightning and sounds and
peals of thunder</u>. And there were seven lamps of fire burning
before the throne, which are the seven Spirits of God; (Rev. 4:5).

Left-brained persons such as I prefer to have things neatly and logically fit together. For a very long time, I assumed that the seals, trumpets,
and bowls are consecutive in their execution, but it becomes obvious that
they are not. Then I thought that they might be concurrent, with the first
seal covering the same time and events as the first trumpet and the first
bowl. That was even more conflicting. In desperation, I even tried to
imagine them in some sort of spatial relationship, with some judgments
folding back upon those that were earlier in time. A satisfactory solution
came to me while studying the Olivet discourse, as I realized that Jesus
gave His disciples an introductory overview of the end times before pro-
ceeding with a more focused discussion of the Tribulation and the
Kingdom (figure 4-1). I believe that the seals serve as that type of
overview in these judgments, see figure 5-1.
Seven seals on the outside of the scroll prevented John and everyone
else from discovering its contents. Then John had seven visions of the
seventieth week of Daniel as the Lamb broke each seal in turn. When the

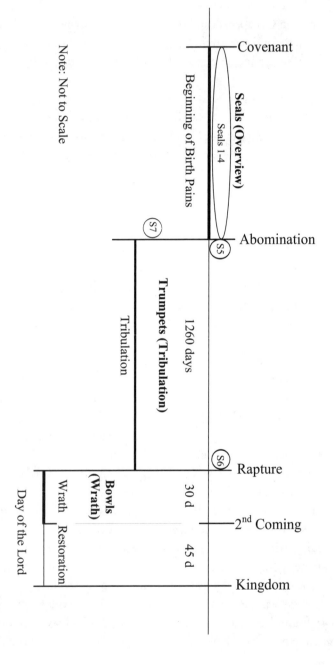

Note: Not to Scale

Figure 5-1, The Judgments of Revelation

last seal was removed, the scroll could finally be read. As the scroll was unwound, the events of the Tribulation were revealed in the seven Trumpet Judgments, one by one and in order. As Paul plainly told the Corinthian church, the Rapture will come at the last, or seventh, trumpet. Finally, with the church removed from the earth, God's Wrath is poured out upon the people of the earth in the form of the seven Bowl Judgments, concluding with the second coming of the Lord Jesus to the spot where He last stood when He ascended from the Mount of Olives.

The Seal and the Trumpet Judgments are similar in the way they are presented. We are shown four seals (or trumpets) that are similar in nature, followed by two seals (or trumpets) that are unlike the first four, with a distinct break in the narration (which many call a parenthesis) before the final seal (or trumpet). The parenthesis provides a pause for the explanation of material that has just been presented, the introduction of new material, or a setup for what is to come.

While the Bowl Judgments do not follow this pattern, we note that the first four bowls have been highlighted above the last three in this statement, "And he said with a loud voice, 'Fear God, and give Him glory, because the hour of His judgment has come; and worship Him who made the heaven [bowl 4] and the earth [bowl 1] and sea [bowl 2] and springs of waters [bowl 3]' " (Rev. 14:7).

THE SEAL JUDGMENTS (REV. 6:1-8:5)

In John's day, a book was a roll of sheepskin or papyrus secured by cloth ribbons or leather strings. When a scroll contained important or proprietary information, it often had one or more seals fastening the string to the papyrus where it overlapped, and only certain people were authorized to remove the seals to read the contents. This scroll was the written record of the events of the Tribulation and had an unusual number of seals.

In general, a seal started as a warm ball of wax that was flattened when impressed with an engraved instrument, often a signet ring unique to the originator. As the wax cooled, it bonded to the scroll and string, became brittle, and had to be broken to remove the string. It was obvious to any observer that this scroll had seven seals that only the slain Lamb of God was worthy to break. As the seals were broken, John had a series of visions about the seventieth week.

The visions of the first four seals seem to parallel those things that Jesus described in the Olivet discourse as the "beginning of birth pains (pangs, or sorrows)." They would therefore occur in the first half of Daniel's seventieth week. This is what Jesus taught:

> Watch that no one deceives you. For many will come in my name, claiming, 'I am the Christ,' and will deceive many. You will hear of wars and rumors of wars, but see to it that you are not alarmed. Such things must happen, but the end is still to come. Nation will rise against nation, and kingdom against kingdom. There will be famines and earthquakes in various places. All these are the beginning of birth pains.
>
> Then you will be handed over to be persecuted and put to death, and you will be hated..." (Matt. 24:4-9).

And this is John's record of his vision of the first four seals:

> And I looked, and behold, a white horse, and he who sat on it had a bow; and a crown was given to him; and he went out conquering, and to conquer.
>
> And when He broke the second seal, I heard the second living creature saying, "Come." And another, a red horse, went out; and to him who sat on it, it was granted to take peace from the earth, and that men should slay one another; and a great sword was given to him.
>
> And when He broke the third seal, I heard the third living creature saying, "Come." And I looked, and behold, a black horse; and he who sat on it had a pair of scales in his hand. And I heard as it were a voice in the center of the four living creatures saying, "A quart of wheat for a denarius, and three quarts of barley for a denarius; and do not harm the oil and the wine."
>
> And when He broke the fourth seal, I heard the voice of the

fourth living creature saying, "Come." And I looked, and behold, an ashen horse; and he who sat on it had the name Death; and Hades was following with him. And authority was given to them over a fourth of the earth, to kill with sword and with famine and with pestilence and by the wild beasts of the earth (Rev. 6:2-8).

Jesus told the disciples that there would be wars between kingdoms and wars between nations. (The Greek word for nation is *ethnos*, from which we get our English word ethnic, characterizing race, religion, or other distinguishing attributes.) John was careful to point out that the rider of the white horse was wearing a crown, indicating his status as a king, but the rider on the red horse was not said to have a crown. Still, this rider did have a "great" sword, with the power to take peace from the earth and to cause men to slay men. We are seeing this principle being exercised in the Middle East even now, as terrorists without borders or a capitol are fighting with recognized countries.

The rider of the third horse carries balance scales and announces grain market prices. The prices quoted are very high, implying a shortage of food, as one would expect during a war when farmers are warriors and invaders are destroying crops and infrastructure. It is only natural that famine would follow. (Note that only annual crops are burned. A voice warns this rider not to harm the (Olive) oil or wine, both of which are derived from mature perennial plants.)

When the Lamb breaks the fourth seal, Death comes on a pale horse with power to kill by sword, famine, plague, and wild beasts. (These are recurring judgments in Scripture.) Hell "follows with him," apparently riding in tandem with him.

And when He broke the fifth seal, I saw underneath the altar the souls of those who had been slain because of the word of God, and because of the testimony which they had maintained; and they cried out with a loud voice, saying, "How long, O Lord, holy and true, wilt Thou refrain from judging and avenging our blood on those who dwell on the earth?" And there was given to each of them a white robe; and they were told that they should rest for a little while longer, until the number of their fellow servants and their brethren who were to be killed even as they had been, should be completed also (Rev. 6:9-11).

When the fifth Seal is broken, John is shown a number of souls under the altar in heaven. From what they say, they are the souls of believers who will have been martyred for their testimonies, from Steven in the early church to the Abomination in the middle of the seventieth week. They are each given a white robe and told that their deaths will not be avenged until many more are killed in the Tribulation. The fifth seal may be considered a snapshot taken at the beginning of the Tribulation.

The sixth seal is another snapshot, this time taken at the end of the Tribulation. It describes three things: the same celestial signs that Jesus described in the Olivet discourse as coming after the Tribulation, the fear and shame of the wicked when they see His Coming, and a proclamation of the arrival of the Wrath of God.

"I watched as he opened the sixth seal. There was a great earthquake. The sun turned black like sackcloth made of goat hair, the whole moon turned blood red, and the stars in the sky fell to earth... The sky receded like a scroll, rolling up, and every mountain and island was removed from its place. Then the kings of the earth, the princes, the generals, the rich, the mighty, and every slave and every free man hid...hide us from the face of him who sits on the throne and from the wrath of the Lamb! For the great day of their wrath has come..." (Rev. 6:12-17)

The vision of the sixth seal describes the signs of the Coming of the Lord, but not those things that actually take place at His Coming, such as the Resurrection and Rapture. These are described where they properly belong, at the end of the Trumpet Judgments.

First Parenthesis

After the sixth seal, we encounter the first of the interruptions in the
story line, often called parentheses, which allows an author to tidy up a
story jammed with diverse facts. In this interlude the message of the
angel is, "Do not harm the land or the sea or the trees UNTIL WE PUT
A SEAL ON THE FOREHEADS OF THE SERVANTS OF OUR
GOD." On one level, the parenthesis shows God's protection of His
people, but on another level, it prevents the first four trumpet judgments, which actually do inflict tremendous damage to the earth and sea,
from being sounded until the servants are sealed (Rev. 7:1-8).

The parenthesis continues with a vision of a robed multitude, "who
have come out of the Great Tribulation," standing before the Lamb.
These are the answer to the remark of the fifth seal, when the souls under
the altar were told to wait until "the number of their fellow servants and
brothers who were to be killed as they had been was completed" (Rev.
6:11). This is the end of the Tribulation, and all of the martyred saints
have been given their robes and worship God, but the church will not be
raptured until the seventh trumpet.

Interestingly, nothing happens when the seventh seal is broken.
Literally, only silence marks the occasion, which may be an indication of
the awe that is inspired by the seven trumpets that are about to reveal the
contents of the scroll. Technically, the Seal Judgments do not end until
Revelation 8:5, with the lightning, thunder, and another earthquake.

THE TRUMPET JUDGMENTS (REV. 8:6-11:19)

The 144,000 righteous Jewish men were marked for their preservation in
the parenthesis of the seals, so the restriction against harming the earth is
lifted, and the earth is indeed assaulted in the first four trumpet judgments. The first trumpet allows hail, fire, and blood to fall to the earth,
causing one-third of the earth and trees and *all* of the grass to be burned
up. The second trumpet is sounded and a fiery mass is thrown (not
"falls") into the sea. Following the pattern of the other trumpets, one-
third of the sea becomes blood, one-third of the life in the sea is choked
out, and one-third of the ships are destroyed.

John is not saying that this will affect all the seas of the earth. John was on the island of Patmos when he wrote the Revelation, and when he made reference to "the sea" (always singular), it was to the Mediterranean Sea surrounding Patmos. When Luke wrote about the travels of the apostle Paul in the book of Acts, his references are also to the Mediterranean Sea. But when the gospels referred to "the sea" either directly or by implication, it usually meant the Sea of Galilee, but occasionally it was the Dead Sea.

The third trumpet summons a blazing star called "Wormwood" (bitter) that poisons one-third of the fresh waters. But people become thirsty and in desperation drink the water even though they know that the bitterness is there, and many die.[26]

At the fourth trumpet, something happens to prevent the sun, moon, and stars from being seen for one-third of the day (or night). Do not confuse this blackout with heavenly signs that precede the Day of the Lord, because the latter are not intermittent and because it is not yet the appointed time for Jesus' coming.

An eagle (angel—KJV) is seen flying through the air, announcing that the next three trumpets will bring "woes" to the inhabitants of the earth, i.e., the unsaved. At the fifth trumpet, the first woe, a "star" falls from heaven, but this star is addressed as "him." This messenger from heaven is given the key to the abyss, presumably the same "bottomless pit" that will confine Satan for a thousand years. When it is opened, a swarm of strange locusts, looking like a cloud of smoke, emerges. They have a king named "Destroyer." These creatures have weapons that will incapacitate men with pain for six months, but without killing them.[27] At this moment, several government entities are developing non-lethal weapons for the military, but no weapon I have read about matches this described in the Bible, but then, why would they tell us?

Here is proof that the Trumpet Judgments cover a substantial amount of time. Notice that the "locusts" are forbidden to harm the grass. Since all grass was burned up in the first trumpet judgment, we know that enough time has passed for there to be a new crop of grass.

The sixth trumpet is the second woe. When it is sounded, a voice from the altar instructs him to release four other angels who had been bound at the Euphrates River. When they are loosed, two hundred million horses and riders charge forth. The horses have heads like lions and they breathe out fire, smoke, and brimstone to kill one-third of mankind. If this means one-third of all people globally, it could be two billion souls. If it means one-third of people in the Middle East region, the number would be substantially less, but still a huge slaughter. The purpose of this judgment is to cause people to repent, but the witness is, that they do not.

Second Parenthesis

Just as in the Seal Judgments, there is a parenthesis after the sixth judgment. First, an angel appears, placing one foot on the land (signifying Israel) and one on the sea (signifying the Gentiles). He has a scroll in his hand, and he cries out with a voice like a roaring lion. The seven thunders we discussed earlier "speak," but when they do, John is told not to record what they say, postponing their messages for the end-time. The message of the next angel is that the mystery of God will end with the seventh trumpet.

John, like Ezekiel of old, is told to eat the scroll the angel was carrying. It tastes sweet, but it also gives him a stomach ache. John was told that he must prophesy again, which could be an indication that he may be one of the two witnesses that are described immediately following this (Rev. 11).

The third thing in this parenthesis is for John to measure the temple, the altar, and those who worship in it (Does he mean "count them"?). But he is told not to measure the court outside the temple, because it would be defiled for forty-two months by Gentiles trespassing upon it. Luke 21:24 says that the Gentiles will trample Jerusalem "until the Times of the Gentiles be fulfilled."

What are "the Times of the Gentiles"? Obviously it is a time when they dominate the Jews, but to what extent and for how long? Many expositors date the Times of the Gentiles from the Babylonian Exile, because from that time on, Israel was subservient to some Gentile nation or other, e.g., the Babylonians, the Greeks, the Romans, and then the

Diaspora that scattered them throughout the world. If serving under a foreign king were the criteria, then one would think that this would have ended when Israel became a nation in 1948, except that two-thirds of Jews are still residing in some country other than Israel. Others say that the Times of the Gentiles began with the destruction of the temple in AD 70 when a large number of Jews were scattered around the world (the Diaspora), and that it will end when the Jews are re-gathered in Daniel's seventieth week. This passage, the only one that contains this phrase, seems to imply that the Times of the Gentiles are these forty-two months.

THE TWO WITNESSES (REV. 11:3-13)

The two witnesses are intriguing both for their behavior in their short ministry as well as the circumstances of their deaths. Even their identity has been a subject of speculation, but no one knows who they are by name. These two can call down fire from heaven, withhold rain from the earth, and release all manner of plagues to torment the wicked. They cannot be killed until the end of the appointed time of their ministry.

While the witnesses perform these miracles, the Beast from the Land (the False Prophet) also calls down fire and performs signs and wonders on behalf of the Beast from the Sea (the Antichrist). Jesus said that people would be supernaturally deceived during this time, so that they would not believe to be saved. The miracles performed by the False Prophet are an example of the nature of the deception.

Just three and one-half days before the 1,260 days are complete, the witnesses will be killed. Their bodies will lie on a street of Jerusalem and the whole world will be able to look upon them, thanks to technology we have had only since 1978.[28] The unsaved will celebrate the deaths of the two who tormented them by exchanging gifts and sending greetings to one another. At the end of the three and one-half days, the witnesses come to life while the world watches, receive new bodies, and ascend to heaven when a shout calls them up. This is the first general resurrection of the righteous.[29] Paul told the church that Jesus was the first fruits of this resurrection, and that all who are called by his name would be raised at a later time, "when He comes." This is in keeping with all other Scriptures regarding the Coming, but especially the words of Jesus in the Olivet discourse.

Immediately, the seventh trumpet is heard calling the living saints to meet Christ in the air. (The shout of the angel is for the dead in Christ; the trumpet is for the living.)

> The seventh angel sounded his trumpet, and there were loud voices in heaven, which said: "The kingdom of the world has become the kingdom of our Lord and of his Christ, and he will reign for ever and ever."
>
> And the twenty-four elders, who were seated on their thrones before God, fell on their faces and worshiped God, saying:
>
> "We give thanks to you, Lord God Almighty, the One who is and who was, because you have taken your great power and have begun to reign. The nations were angry; and your wrath has come. The time has come for judging the dead, and for rewarding your servants the prophets and your saints and those who reverence your name, both small and great—and for destroying those who destroy the earth" (Rev. 11:15-18 NIV).

INTRA-JUDGMENT PARENTHESIS (REV. 12-14)

A number of things important to the understanding of the Revelation are presented in the three chapters between the Rapture and the Wrath of God (Bowl Judgments). Chapter 12 portrays Satan (the Dragon) opposing Israel (the woman), Jesus (her child), and the church (her other offspring). The metaphor confirms that the saints will be nourished in the wilderness for the 1,260 days of the Tribulation.

Chapter 13 tells us much of what we know about the Antichrist (Beast from the Sea, a Gentile), and the False Prophet (Beast from the earth, a Jew). The first ten verses confirm the "little horn" of the vision of Daniel 7, with specific information about the death and resurrection of the Antichrist. The remaining verses give us details about the programs that the False Prophet will introduce during the Tribulation, the glorification of the Antichrist, the Abomination, and the Mark of the Beast.

Revelation 14 tells us that the 144,000 chaste Jews will follow Jesus wherever He goes, and that they sing a song that no other person can sing. We are told that the seal with which they were sealed on the forehead are the names of God the Father and God the Son. A series of seven angels appear, including the one that proclaims the gospel throughout the world, one that announces the fall of Babylon, another who tells the fate of any who worship the Beast and take his mark, the Son of Man who harvests the righteous out of the earth, and another angel who harvests the wicked to wrath.

THE BOWL JUDGMENTS (REV. 15-16)

We have just seen how the testimony of Paul in the first Corinthian letter will be fulfilled regarding the "dead in Christ" joining Jesus in the clouds, followed by "those who are alive and remaining." The period called the Tribulation is over, and the Day of the Lord begins with these Bowl Judgments. As if to complement the descriptions of the contents of these bowls being dispersed quickly, the Greek word for the bowls describes a wide, shallow pan rather than a jar. The punishments of the bowls on the earth's inhabitants are justified in Revelation fifteen and executed in chapter sixteen.

The angel holding the first bowl scatters the contents over the earth and all the people who worshiped the Antichrist and received his mark are smitten with "loathsome and malignant sores," perhaps similar to the Ebola plague.

You may recall that the second Trumpet Judgment affected one-third of the waters in the sea. Now the second bowl is thrown upon the sea, turning all of the waters to blood and killing every creature living in it. Imagine the smell from the rotting carcasses as they float to the surface.

The third bowl is cast upon streams and rivers that supply fresh water to drink, cook, and bathe. The waters become blood and the angels declare this to be a proper judgment for men who spilled the blood of the saints and Prophets.

The contents of the fourth bowl are flung toward the sun, and men are scorched with great heat. These judgments are not inflicted upon the inhabitants of the earth to get them to repent. It is too late for that. This is the righteous wrath of God being administered to those who have rejected Him even though they have known the truth and the way. Again I will remind you that there will not be one Saint present to feel this heat.

The fifth bowl is poured on the throne of the Beast and extreme darkness falls upon his kingdom. I struggle to understand the physics that result in such a phenomena. When Moses plagued Egypt and God sent darkness upon the land, it was described as darkness "that could be felt" (Exodus 10:21-23). How far will the darkness extend? We don't know if only his civic centers are affected, or if it will envelop the city or country in which he is situated. In Moses' time, it affected all of Egypt except for the region where the Israelites lived.

Bowl six is directed to the Euphrates River, which waters are dried up to give the kings of the East access to Jerusalem. Unclean spirits come out of the mouths of Satan, the Antichrist, and the False Prophet, and these go to the kings of the whole earth to gather their armies to a site north-west of Jerusalem. Without knowing it, they are doing exactly what God wants them to do in preparation for the final war before Christ's Kingdom is established. The staging of the battle of Armageddon is being set for the Second Coming in the middle of the Day of the Lord.

Tremendous changes in the topology of the earth take place in preparation of the Kingdom when the seventh bowl is poured into the air (Isa. 40:4). A great earthquake splits "the great city (Rome or Babylon)" in three parts. Other cities will be flattened, mountains leveled, and the islands disappear (Rev. 16:19-21). One hundred pound hailstones fall from the skies to punish mankind for their opposition to the plan of God. The time of these phenomena seemingly coincides with the second coming of Christ, when the Mount of Olives splits north and south (Zech.14:3-5).

The judgment of Babylon is described in the next two chapters of the Revelation. It is highly symbolic and beyond the purpose of this book for commentary.

The things we have discussed in this chapter are very frightening for the unsaved person, as they should be. And the scariest part is not the suffering and pain that will come upon them, but the reality of eternal separation from God. In the days of the Tribulation, a strong delusion will come upon all who have rejected the salvation that was offered them in the days of grace, so that there will be no repentance, even in the midst of punishment. You who are resisting the call of the Holy Spirit to salvation must give up the fantasy that you will do it on your deathbed or when things start getting rough.

You must call upon God to save you, in Jesus' name. What does that mean? It means that you acknowledge Jesus as God's only son, who came in human flesh to live a holy life and to die as the sacrifice necessary to cover your sins. Yes, that is a very narrow view, but it is the truth as revealed in God's Word, the Bible. Do it now and let Him transform your life.

The material in this chapter does not cover all of that which the book of Revelation has to say about end times. In truth, it is probably inexhaustible!

6

The Antichrist

It is human nature to be intrigued by an unresolved mystery, a word puzzle, a large construction project, gossip, and other incomplete business. We love to find a solution, fill in the blanks, direct the action, or name the villain. In this chapter, we are going to piece together information concerning the man who will fulfill prophecies of Daniel, Paul, Peter, John, and others. This person is variously called in Scripture "the little horn" (Daniel 7:8), "the prince who is to come" (Dan. 9:26), "a vile person" (Dan. 11:21), "the man of sin" (2 Thess. 2:3), "the Beast from the Sea," (Rev. 13:1), "the Beast from the bottomless pit" (Rev. 11:7; 17:8), "a Scarlet Beast full of blasphemous names" (Rev. 17:3), and "the antichrist" (1 John 2:18). Since we don't know his birth name, we will simply call him by his title, "the Antichrist." We will capitalize his title, not out of respect, but because he will be a prominent unique individual in days to come.

FATE OF THE ANTICHRIST

It should comfort us, that in every major passage of the Bible concerning the Antichrist, a statement is included that his destiny has already been determined. Some of the references to his fate are Daniel 7:11, "I kept looking until the beast was slain, and its body was destroyed and given to the burning fire." or its interpretation, "But the court will sit for judgment, and his dominion will be taken away, annihilated and destroyed forever (v26)." Also in Daniel 9:27, "…until a complete destruction, one that is decreed, is poured out on the one who makes desolate." and Daniel 11:45, "…yet he will come to his end, and no one will help him." Paul said in 2 Thessalonians 2:8, "Whom the Lord will slay with the breath of His mouth and bring to an end by the appearance of His coming." John had a vision in Revelation 19:20 in which "these two (the Antichrist and the False Prophet) were thrown alive into the lake of fire which burns with brimstone."

GENERAL FACTS ABOUT THE ANTICHRIST

There are several Bible passages that describe some characteristic of the man who carries so many names, but there is no one passage that describes him in all aspects of his personality, accomplishments, ambitions, etc. You may be familiar with the fable of the blind men who encountered an elephant for the first time, but each man touched only a part of the animal. The one who grabbed the tail said it was like a rope. The elephant's leg was likened to a tree, his trunk to a fire hose, his ears to wings, and his side to a wall. If you read only one or two passages concerning the Antichrist, you will learn some truths about him, but you won't have "the big picture." By the time we are through with this chapter, I hope that you have a better understanding of the person and program of the Antichrist.

In his letters, John acknowledged the coming of the Antichrist, but said that there would be many antichrists, which he defined as "anyone that denies the Father and the Son." The spirit of antichrist is already present in the person of anyone who denies Christ (1 John 2:18; 2:22; 4:3; 2 John 1:7). Still, there will be one unique man who will embody that denial.

When the Antichrist appears on the world scene, he will be a human being, having a body, soul, and spirit like you and I, so we assume that he will be born of a woman, nurtured and educated as a child, and he will mature to the adult we first see. He will be brilliant and charismatic, able to win the confidence, if not the admiration, of most people. The only thing we are told about his appearance is that he will have a stern look (fierce countenance) (Dan. 8:23 KJV). Within a few years of coming upon the world scene, he will consolidate the powers of ten other kings, but he will not be revealed to the world as the Antichrist until the covenant has been in place for almost three and one-half years. At that time, he "takes his seat in the temple of God, displaying himself as being God" (2 Thess. 2:4).

This man is probably already alive on earth, perhaps as a child or an adolescent, but somewhere along the development path we just laid out. Our reasons for making that statement will be explained in the next chapter.

When this man is revealed to be the Antichrist, he will have a precisely defined period of time to exercise his authority. Daniel was told that "they [the saints] will be given into his hand for a time, times, and half a time [that is, three and one-half years]" (Dan. 7:25). By the end of that predetermined period, the power of the holy people will have been broken, that is, they will have no means by which they can resist him (Dan. 8:24; 12:7). By God's sovereign will, they may be hidden in the wilderness, or imprisoned, or killed for their testimony. This may also be a reference to the fact that the two witnesses, who are the only significant public opposition the Antichrist will have, will finally be killed. If he were allowed any more time, no believers would survive in the flesh (Matt. 24:22).

The Antichrist will not present himself as the Jewish Messiah, but as an alternative to the Messiah, and not just to the Jews but for all people. The apostates to whom Jesus and Paul referred (Matt. 24:10-11, 24; 2 Thess. 2:3) will obviously know that he is an imitator; otherwise they would not be called "apostates," who by definition, must renounce their profession of the true Messiah for the fake.

A favorite activity of Christians familiar with prophecy, especially in the last hundred years or more, has been guessing the identity of the Antichrist. They have taken their clues from the same passages that we are considering, but some have also appropriated Bible passages to apply to him that do not concern him at all. Therefore, virtually any well-known man could be named as the Antichrist by some commentator or other.

Daniel 9:26 says that *"the people of the prince who is to come will destroy the city and the sanctuary…"* We know that the Roman army destroyed the city and temple in AD 70, so we have every right to suggest that the Antichrist will be Italian.[30] On the other hand, the Romans conquered many countries in Europe and the Middle East, so we have to leave open the possibility that he could be of some other nationality or race.[31] One could make the argument that he could come from the United States of America, because it was founded by people who came from countries once controlled by Rome. Attempts to identify him at this time may be futile, because he will only be positively identified when God allows him to reveal himself toward the middle of the week (2 Thess. 2:3-8).

THE TWO "LITTLE HORNS"

The key to understanding the origins of the Antichrist depends upon understanding two visions Daniel had, about two significant men and how they interrelate with one another. In these visions, he saw them as "little horns."

The terms "horn" and "horns" are used throughout Scripture in several ways, but it is obvious from the contexts which meaning is intended wherever it is found. Obviously, there is the ordinary use as it applies to horned animals. Scores of times "horns" refers to the four protrusions on the corners of the sacrificial altar. But the word is also used symbolically for the strength and exalted position of an individual.

The beasts of prophetic visions, representing countries or political systems, are depicted as having a horn or several horns that represent kings and leaders. Horns used this way could be little (weak) or great (strong). They are said to grow (become stronger), or to be plucked out of their place (removed from power), or broken (killed). In one vision, the horn was said to have eyes and a mouth to speak.

Prior to the vision of the seventy weeks, these two visions came to the elderly Daniel about two years apart. Both came at a transition of gentile rulers over Israel, reassuring Daniel that the Lord was in control of Israel's future. One vision concerned the coming Antichrist at the end of the "present age," and the other was about a Greek ruler who was presented as a living "type" of the Antichrist. The ruler was Antiochus IV, who lived one and one-half centuries before Christ, and who fulfilled many, but not all, of the prophecies of the Antichrist.

The First "Little Horn," The Antichrist

Very early in Daniel's exile in Babylon, he was called upon to divine a dream that the King of Babylon had, and then to interpret that dream (Dan. 2:1-45). The interpretation described gentile nations that would rule over the Jews, from Nebuchadnezzar to the end of the age.

About fifty years later, in the first year of the reign of a new Babylonian king, Daniel had a second vision, also about future world rulers. As you would expect, it had no reference to the late Nebuchadnezzar, but it introduced a blasphemous person who will appear in the last days, when a ten-nation federation would dominate the world. This is the first Bible prophecy that describes the Antichrist in any detail. The reader is urged to become familiar with the whole chapter, but we pick it up in the middle of the vision:

> After this I kept looking in the night visions, and behold, a fourth beast [Rome], dreadful and terrifying and extremely strong; and it had large iron teeth. It devoured and crushed, and trampled down the remainder with its feet; and it was different from all the beasts that were before it, and it had ten horns [The future kingdom]. While I was contemplating the horns, behold, another horn, a little one, [Antichrist] came up among them, and three of the first horns were pulled out by the roots before it; and behold, this horn possessed eyes like the eyes of a man, and a mouth uttering great boasts" (Dan. 7:7-8).

Daniel asked the angel about the striking fierceness of the fourth kingdom, and of the ten kings, and the nature of the little horn that comes from among them. The angel answered:

> The fourth beast will be a fourth kingdom on the earth, which will be different from all the other kingdoms, and it will devour the

whole earth and tread it down and crush it. As for the ten horns, out of this kingdom ten kings will arise; and another will arise after them, and he will be different from the previous ones and will subdue three kings. And he will speak out against the Most High and wear down the saints of the Highest One, and he will intend to make alterations in times and in law; and they will be given into his hand for a time, times, and half a time [three and one-half years or forty-two months or 1,260 days] (Dan. 7:23-25).

The fourth kingdom was the Roman Empire, now considered to have passed from the world scene, but in the future, ten kings will rise from the remnants of the Empire and join together in a loose alliance and be considered a single entity. The Antichrist will not be one of the ten kings, but he will somehow be a product of this alliance. He will be at odds with three of the ten, even to the point that he will subdue them, but apparently he will allow them to continue in power, because the number of kings that swear allegiance to the Antichrist are said to be ten whenever they are mentioned.

In the interpretation, Daniel was told that the Antichrist will speak arrogantly against God and that the saints will be subject to him for three and one-half years, during which time he "wears them down." He will seek to eliminate the Jewish observances (laws, feasts, and holidays) and to change the appointed times that God has decreed (v. 25). The vision ends with the ultimate outcome:

Then the sovereignty, the dominion, and the greatness of all the kingdoms under the whole heaven will be given to the people of the saints of the Highest One; His kingdom will be an everlasting kingdom, and all the dominions will serve and obey Him. (Dan. 7:27).

The Second "Little Horn," Antiochus IV

About two years after the first vision, Daniel had another in which he saw two beasts fighting with each other. The interpretation of these beasts is given a little later in the chapter, even to naming the kingdoms they represent.

> While I was observing, behold, a male goat [Greece, v.21] was coming from the west over the surface of the whole earth without touching the ground; and the goat had a conspicuous horn between his eyes. And he came up to the ram that had the two horns [Medo-Persia, v.20], which I had seen standing in front of the canal, and rushed at him in his mighty wrath. And I saw him come beside the ram, and he was enraged at him; and he struck the ram and shattered his two horns, and the ram had no strength to withstand him. So he hurled him to the ground and trampled on him, and there was none to rescue the ram from his power. Then the male goat magnified himself exceedingly. But as soon as he was mighty, the large horn was broken; and in its place there came up four conspicuous horns toward the four winds of heaven (Dan. 8:5-8).

The "prominent horn" of the goat undoubtedly referred to Alexander the Great, who conquered the civilized world by the time he was thirty years of age. He died of alcoholism when still a young man, and since he had no heirs, four of his generals divided up the conquered lands and assumed the rule over them. The parcel that included the land of Israel, called Seleucid, was taken by Antiochus. A succession of his male descendants inherited the rule, down to the one who is the subject of this prophecy, Antiochus IV, who called himself Antiochus Epiphanes (God Manifest).

> And out of one of them came forth a rather small horn [Antiochus Epiphanes] which grew exceedingly great toward the south, toward the east, and toward the Beautiful Land [Israel]. And it grew up to the host of heaven and caused some of the host and some of the stars [angels] to fall to the earth, and it trampled them down. It even magnified itself to be equal with the Commander of the host [The Son of God]; and it removed the regular sacrifice

from Him, and the place of His sanctuary was thrown down. And on account of transgression the host [the Elect, the saints] will be given over to the horn along with the regular sacrifice; and it will fling truth to the ground and perform its will and prosper. Then I heard a holy one [angel] speaking, and another holy one said to that particular one who was speaking, "How long will the vision about the regular sacrifice apply, while the transgression causes horror, so as to allow both the holy place and the host to be trampled?" And he said to me, "For 2,300 evenings and mornings; then the holy place will be properly restored" (Dan. 8:9-14).

The life of Antiochus Epiphanes is well documented in secular histories. To achieve his status as king, he had to murder the rightful king, who was his older brother, and seized the kingdom from his nephew, who was in Rome at the time. While he then successfully conquered lands around him, he held a hatred for, and often harassed, the Jews. Israel had been subservient to Greece for many years, and much of the Greek culture had been absorbed into Jewish society, to the shame of the religious orthodox citizens. Around 168 BC, Antiochus auctioned the office of high priest, and the high bidder bought his position with golden utensils from the temple. Without these cups and bowls, the offerings could not be properly administered for 2300 days.

A few years later, he was turned away in battle by the king of the South. On his return home, the humiliated Antiochus desecrated the Jewish temple by erecting an altar to Zeus and sacrificing a pig on the altar. He boiled the flesh of the swine and splattered the broth over the temple and its furnishings. This was an "abomination that makes desolate," but it was not the one Jesus said would desecrate the temple in the end time.

His persecution of the Jews became more and more intense until the family of Joseph Maccabaeus rose up in opposition to the Greeks. He and his sons seized control of Jerusalem exactly three years after the abomination and cleansed the temple so it could again be used for ritual sacrifices. The 2300 days ended when the ritual sanctification of the temple was complete. The Jews mark this event with the celebration of Hanukkah in December of every year.

While history verifies that many of the things Daniel saw in this vision have been fulfilled, we find that not all of them were. Gabriel appeared to Daniel to add these words:

"Son of man, understand that the vision pertains to the time of the end." Now while he was talking with me, I sank into a deep sleep with my face to the ground; but he touched me and made me stand upright. And he said, "Behold, I am going to let you know what will occur at the final period of the indignation, for it pertains to the appointed time of the end" (Dan. 8:17-19).

And in the latter period of their rule, when the transgressors have run their course, a king will arise Insolent and skilled in intrigue. And his power will be mighty, but not by his own power, and he will destroy to an extraordinary degree and prosper and perform his will; he will destroy mighty men and the holy people. And through his shrewdness he will cause deceit to succeed by his influence; and he will magnify himself in his heart, and he will destroy many while they are at ease. He will even oppose the Prince of princes, but he will be broken without human agency.

And the vision of the evenings and mornings which has been told is true; but keep the vision secret, for it pertains to many days in the future (Dan. 8:23-26).

MERGER OF ANTIOCHUS AND THE ANTICHRIST

A summary of what we have just read may be helpful at this point.

It would appear from the table below that these men have nothing in common, except for a hatred of the Jews. However, there is an intimate joining of the two as they converge in the end time, one that is not obvious. The answer was given to John in the Revelation. What I am about to say will sound very, very strange, but it is an inescapable conclusion based upon harmony of the Scriptures. I cannot claim any originality for it, but neither can I tell you where I first heard it.

Name:	Antichrist	Antiochus
Reference:	Daniel ch 7	Daniel ch 8
Ancestry:	No royalty	Seleucid dynasty
Background:	From among 10 kings	From 1 of 4 kings
Days of Rule:	1,260	2,300
Time of Rule:	70th week of Daniel	2nd century BC

Figure 6-1, Comparison of the Little Horns

In the Revelation, John saw a vision of a harlot in purple and red garments, riding upon a Scarlet Beast that has seven heads and ten horns. (Keep in mind that this is a representation of a reality we must try to understand.) The symbols of the seven heads and ten horns are explained in the context, but it is the *beast* upon which we now need to focus.

> The beast that you saw was and is not, and is about to come up out of the abyss and to go to destruction. And those who dwell on the earth will wonder, whose name has not been written in the book of life from the foundation of the world, when they see the beast, that he was and is not and will come (Rev. 17:8)

> Twice, John was told that the Beast *was* (he lived before this), *is not* (he was not alive when John wrote this), and *will come* (he will live again in the end times). We know from Scripture that every person dies in the flesh, but his soul and spirit lives on. We have to ask ourselves, "What man lived and died before AD 95 (the time John wrote this), and was so wicked that Satan would want him revived in the end times to carry on his evil work?" You may go down the list of kings and despots, but I don't think that you will find a better candidate than the one who called himself "God Manifest," Antiochus IV. Could the man that lived 160 years before Christ actually be the same man who is described as the future Beast from the Sea? The description of the Antichrist hints at how this might be accomplished.

And he [The Dragon] stood on the sand of the seashore. And I saw a beast coming up out of the sea, having ten horns and seven heads, and on his horns were ten diadems, and on his heads were blasphemous names. And the beast which I saw was like a leopard, and his feet were like those of a bear, and his mouth like the mouth of a lion. And the dragon gave him his power and his throne and great authority.

And I saw one of his heads as if it had been slain, and his fatal wound was healed. And the whole earth was amazed and followed after the beast; and they worshiped the dragon, because he gave his authority to the beast; and they worshiped the beast, saying, "Who is like the beast, and who is able to wage war with him?" And there was given to him a mouth speaking arrogant words and blasphemies; and authority to act for forty-two months was given to him. And he opened his mouth in blasphemies against God, to blaspheme His name and His tabernacle, that is, those who dwell in heaven.

And it was given to him to make war with the saints and to overcome them; and authority over every tribe and people and tongue and nation was given to him. And all who dwell on the earth will worship him, everyone whose name has not been written from the foundation of the world in the book of life of the Lamb who has been slain. If anyone has an ear, let him hear [pay attention and understand this] (Rev. 13:1-9).

The book of Revelation is highly symbolic, but each of the symbols stands for something literal. The Dragon of chapter 12 had seven heads and ten horns, as did this Beast from the Sea and the Scarlet Beast of Revelation 17. When John wrote about the Dragon, the *heads* were wearing crowns, but when the subject was the Beast from the Sea, the *horns* wore crowns. Their close relationship and common roots are revealed in these symbols. We have learned that the ten horns are ten kings who live at the same time. The meaning of the seven heads is found in Revelation 17:10, where they are interpreted as seven kings or empires that ruled over Israel sequentially in their respective eras. The first six kings were

Egypt, Assyria, Babylon, Medo-Persia, Greece, and Rome, with the seventh to be a coalition of ten kings in the last days. The Antichrist will arise in their midst and subsequently take over this last ten-king federation.[32]

> ...and they are seven kings; five have fallen, one is, the other has not yet come; and when he comes, he must remain a little while. And the beast which was and is not, is himself also an eighth, and is one of the seven, and he goes to destruction (Rev. 17:10-11).

One of the heads of the Scarlet Beast will receive a mortal wound. Since this was not true of any of the first six, historically, it must be a reference to the future ruler. The seventh head, the man that emerges from the ten-king coalition, will be killed and his resurrected body will be indwelled with the spirit of Antiochus Epiphanes. It is at this point that the man who has done the bidding of Satan on earth, who signs the covenant at the beginning of the seventieth week, who conquers the ten kings and many nations, becomes the Antichrist. The Antichrist that is described in Daniel 7 did not materially exist until this time. He is no longer the seventh king, but he is now the eighth king of this series, just as the Scarlet Beast was not considered to be one of the seven heads of his body. He is no longer just a clever and cruel leader of men. He now exhibits the characteristics attributed to him by the prophecies of Daniel, i.e., the arrogance, the blasphemies, and the authority over all peoples.

The death and resurrection of the Antichrist mimics our Lord's death and resurrection. When the world sees him raised to life, they worship him and give Satan the credit for his resurrection. This is their excuse to turn away from the Lord God who demands a holy and sanctified life and embrace a champion who will promote a lifestyle of depravity without the restrictions of Judeo-Christian morality. People who have given lip service to God will turn from their profession of Him and become the apostates that Jesus spoke of (Matt. 24:12) and Paul wrote about (2 Thess. 2:3; 9-12).

In full view of his admirers, the Antichrist goes to the Jewish temple in Jerusalem to sit on a throne erected for him, and proclaims himself as

God. The False Prophet commemorates the occasion by erecting an image of the Antichrist in the temple, thereby fulfilling the prophecy of the abomination of desolation. This could not be done without the Restrainer stepping aside (2 Thess. 2:4-9).

We acknowledge that the details of the paragraphs above are not laid out this graphically in the Bible. All of the facts are in the Bible, and this is the only way their relationship can be compatible while holding a literal interpretation.

FROM OBSCURITY TO WORLD LEADER

We have attempted to show how a remarkably wicked man who lived two centuries before Christ will become the Antichrist, fulfilling the prophecies of Daniel 7 and 8. But before the man who will be the Antichrist is filled with the spirit of Antiochus Epiphanes, he will have been a mortal, albeit a wicked man. How does he achieve the notoriety he has when he is killed?

Some time after Daniel was given the instruction of the Seventy Weeks, he engaged in lengthy prayer and meditation, and in response, an angel (we are not told that it is Gabriel) appeared to him again with this message: "Now I have come to give you an understanding of what will happen to your people in the latter days, for the vision pertains to the days yet future" (Dan. 10:14). This is the point in the narrative where I believe the man who will become the Antichrist first appears:

> And in his [the previous king's] place a despicable person [The man who will be Antichrist] will arise, on whom the honor of kingship has not been conferred [he is not from a royal lineage], but he will come in a time of tranquility and seize the kingdom by intrigue [not Israel, but his own country]. And the overflowing forces will be flooded away before him and shattered, and also the prince of the covenant [a Jewish priest or political leader]. And after an alliance is made with him he will practice deception, and he will go up and gain power with a small force of people. In a time of tranquility he will enter the richest parts of the realm

[his country], and he will accomplish what his fathers never did, nor his ancestors; he will distribute plunder, booty, and possessions among them, and he will devise his schemes against strongholds, but only for a time. And he will stir up his strength and courage against the king of the South with a large army; so the king of the South will mobilize an extremely large and mighty army for war; but he [The king of the South] will not stand, for schemes will be devised against him [an internal coup]. And those who eat his choice food will destroy [break] him, and his army will overflow, but many will fall down slain. As for both kings, their hearts will be intent on evil, and they will speak lies to each other at the same table; but it will not succeed, for the end is still to come at the appointed time. Then he will return to his land with much plunder; but his heart will be set against the holy covenant [the Jews], and he will take action and then return to his own land (Dan. 11:21-28).

The man described in this passage does not come from royal lineage, confirming the prophecy of him as the little horn in Daniel 8:9-12. At a time when his country is at peace, he seizes control of it by deception, not by might, but somehow "overflowing forces" of opposition are put down. This is the first of several miracles that propel him to domination.

In this narrative, once this man gains authority, he signs an "alliance" with another country, and deceives them when he reneges on that agreement. In that regard, he prefigures his violation of the covenant at the Abomination. At this point, he has only a small following, but he distributes the wealth he acquires to his few loyal followers. This generosity is not lost on many who are watching him, and soon he has a "large army" to go against larger countries.

The next target is "The king of the South," which is probably not Egypt, because Egypt is specifically named separately later in the chapter. This king meets him with "an extremely large and mighty army," which would normally determine the outcome of the battle, but some of the inner circle sabotage and "break" the king of the South so that the two kings have to negotiate an end of hostilities. The settlement seems to go well for the Antichrist, because he returns home with "much plunder." He also sets his heart against the Holy Covenant, i.e., the Jews.

The prophecies of Daniel do not speak of the death wound of the Antichrist, so we don't know where that comes in this narrative. Clearly it has not yet happened, but it must have happened before the abomination of desolation.

> At the appointed time he will return and come into the South, but this last time it will not turn out the way it did before. For ships of Kittim [Cyprus] will come against him; therefore he will be disheartened, and will return and become enraged at the holy covenant and take action; so he will come back and show regard for those who forsake the holy covenant [apostasy]. And forces from him will arise, desecrate the sanctuary fortress, and do away with the regular sacrifice. And they will set up the abomination of desolation (Dan. 11:29-31).

In the fullness of God's time, the man who will be Antichrist again mounts an attack against the king of the South, but he is turned back by ships based on Cyprus.[33] Now he becomes really angry, and takes out his frustration upon Israel. Whatever military force prevents him from attacking the king of the South, they do not care that he attacks Israel. That reflects the attitude of most of the world today and confirms the prophecy that Israel will have no allies in the last days.

Perhaps it is more accurate to say that this man hates the God of Israel more than he hates the Jews, because this passage shows that he actually rewards Jewish apostates when they turn against the covenant that God has with them. The False Prophet, probably a Jew himself (Rev. 13:14-15), leads his followers in desecrating the temple compound, causing the offering of sacrifices to cease when they set up the abomination of desolation. This marks the middle of the Seventieth week, a most important event on the prophetic calendar. It is the day from which other major events are counted (Dan. 12:7, 11, 12).

We have written about God's "*Restrainer*" that is holding back the Man of Lawlessness, as the apostle Paul calls him. Most people believe that the Antichrist is being restrained from perpetrating the evil he would like to impose upon us, but Paul said that the restraint is there to prevent him from revealing himself before the appointed time, thus confirming the passage above.

> And you know what restrains him now, so that in his time he may be revealed. For the mystery of lawlessness is already at work; only he who now restrains will do so until he is taken out of the way (2 Thess. 2:6-7).

THE ANTICHRIST IN THE TRIBULATION

This book is not being written to graphically present all of the terrible things that will take place in the Tribulation, nor is it our primary purpose to make emotional appeals for people to do the right thing with regard to the will of the Lord. We are trying to present the facts as they are found in the Bible, and to show how those facts relate one to the other.

The abomination of desolation of Daniel 11:31 marks the beginning of the Tribulation. It is the sign given the disciples on the Mount of Olives so they would know that the end of the age was near. There are 1,260 days from this moment until the next key marker, the Resurrection of the righteous and the Rapture of the saints at the last (seventh) trumpet.

> And by smooth words he will turn to godlessness those who act wickedly toward the covenant, but the people who know their God will display strength and take action. And those who have insight among the people will give understanding to the many; yet they will fall by sword and by flame, by captivity and by plunder, for many days. Now when they fall they will be granted a little help, and many will join with them in hypocrisy. And some of those who have insight will fall, in order to refine, purge, and make them pure, until the end time; because it is still to come at the appointed time (Dan. 11:32-35)

In the Tribulation, people have a choice. They can swear fidelity to the Beast and be given a mark (tattoo) that will allow them to engage in commerce, or they can refuse the mark and receive a death penalty. This could be the meaning of verse thirty-two, above. If they take the mark, their names will not be recorded in the Book of Life, and if it was already written there, it will be blotted out. The Revelation tells us several times of punishing disasters that await those who do not have their names in the Book of Life.

Anti-Semitism has been around almost as long as the Jews have been upon the earth. The embarrassment of the Holocaust seemed to have driven much of it underground after WW II, but it has resurfaced, and it is growing. It will be encouraged by the Antichrist in the Tribulation.

The covenant mentioned in this passage is not the document that initiates the final seven years of this age. This covenant is the one that God made with the Jews thousands of years ago. "Those who act wickedly toward the covenant" are those who will persecute the Jews.

Verse thirty-three and Daniel 12:3 tell us that there will be people with "insight" who will impart understanding to many and lead them to righteousness. In spite of this, many will be killed by the forces of the Antichrist to "refine, purge, and make them pure." I'm sure that the need for the refining process is true of the Christian as well as the Jew. They are seen in heaven with white robes in the sixth seal of the Revelation.

The saints of the Tribulation are promised "a little help, and many will join with them in hypocrisy." A hypocrite is one who professes belief in one thing but does another, and in this case it appears that the hypocrite says he honors the Antichrist, while helping the righteous. If so, the motive could only be monetary, because no one who has taken the mark will be redeemed. Another possibility is that this is simply a reference to the existence of a black market in food and commodity items that will sustain some of the saints.

The Mark of the Beast

The program for the Mark of the Beast is found in only one passage in the Revelation. It is apparently devised and administered by the False Prophet to guarantee that all people will worship the Antichrist.

The False Prophet, called "The Beast from the Land," is also empowered by Satan, to be the spokesman for the Antichrist. He is the one who sets up an image of the Antichrist in the Jewish temple. He is the one who administers the program of the mark. The Antichrist decrees that no one can buy or sell anything without displaying a mark of his name or number, and the mark is only given to those who worship an image of the Antichrist.

> And he [the beast from the land] causes all, the small and the great, and the rich and the poor, and the free men and the slaves, to be given a mark on their right hand, or on their forehead, and he provides that no one should be able to buy or to sell, except the one who has the mark, either the name of the beast or the number of his name. Here is wisdom. Let him who has understanding calculate the number of the beast, for the number is that of a man; and his number is six hundred and sixty-six (Rev. 13:16-18).

For a more thorough discussion of the mark, please see chapter two, "The Seventieth Week of Daniel."

The Religion of the Antichrist

Several verses dwell upon the relationship of the Antichrist with any higher being to which he may give homage. Daniel was told earlier (Daniel 7:8, 11, 20) that he would speak terrible things about the true God, and here, that he does not follow the gods (or God) of his ancestry, nor any other god, except....

> Then the king will do as he pleases, and he will exalt and magnify himself above every god, and will speak monstrous things against the God of gods; and he will prosper until the indignation is finished, for that which is decreed will be done. And he will show no regard for the gods of his fathers or for the desire of women, nor will he show regard for any other god; for he will magnify

himself above them all. But instead he will honor a god of fortresses, a god whom his fathers did not know; he will honor him with gold, silver, costly stones, and treasures. And he will take action against the strongest of fortresses with the help of a foreign god; he will give great honor to those who acknowledge him, and he will cause them to rule over the many, and will parcel out land for a price (Dan. 11:36-39).

The only god the Antichrist is said to honor, and he does so lavishly, is one of "fortresses." i.e., a god of defenses.. This god will evidently be a new concept in his time, because it is unknown to the previous generation. This could involve high technology or something of which we have no knowledge.

I feel compelled to refute a teaching that takes the words, "neither shall he regard…the desire of women (KJV)" to claim that the Antichrist will be a homosexual. Keep in mind that this whole passage is dealing with the religion of the Antichrist and nothing else. A better translation might be "he will show no regard for the one desired by women (NIV)." For thousands of years, heathen civilizations have worshiped a female goddess, and even some of Israel got caught up in it. In our day, feminists would like to remove any reference to God having male attributes. It would not surprise me to learn of the existence of a contemporary church that worships such a deity.

The World-Wide Domination of the Antichrist

Lest anyone think that the Antichrist has no enemies in the Tribulation, they should read Daniel 11:40-45. He will conquer many countries, but the king of the South will "collide" with him and the king of the North will "storm against him," and he will be sufficiently disturbed by rumors from the north and east that he will charge off to squelch them.

Yes, the Bible says that the whole world will follow him, but it also tells us there will be many who will not take his mark. The understanding we get from this is that his influence will be felt across over the globe, but it will not be as strong in some places as it will be in others. It may be relatively ineffective in some places. There will be many who will not bow to him, and some of them will be judged, declared to be righteous, and permitted to enter the Millennium.

The Fate of the Antichrist

As we said at the outset of this chapter, the fate of the Antichrist and the False Prophet has been sealed. Their three and one-half year reign of terror ends with the resurrection of the two witnesses and the Rapture of the saints, but they live on to witness and endure the *thumos* Wrath of God in the Bowl Judgments. In a vain attempt to thwart the will of God, they assemble the armies of the nations at Armageddon, only to have them slaughtered by Jesus and the armies of heaven. They will both be thrown into the lake of everlasting burning sulfur. Amen! And Hallelujah!

The lake of fire is an interesting study. Jesus said that it was prepared for "the devil and his angels;" (Matt. 25:41), but that it would also be the destiny of all "whose names are not found in the book of life." (Rev. 20:14, 21:8; Isa. 66:24). That means that you, if you are not saved, will find it your eternal home as well. Please insure yourself a place in heaven after you die, by placing your trust in Jesus, the Son of God, right now.

When Will These Things Be?

The Bible tells us in narration, parables, history, poetry, prophecy, and the direct word, that God knows the future and that nothing comes as a surprise to Him. He has already determined when key events of the end-time will take place. When Daniel was told about the rise of the Antichrist, the phrase "at the appointed time" is used three times (Dan. 11:27, 29, 35). The same phrase, or one with the same meaning, is also found in Daniel 8:19, Habakkuk 2:3, and Zephaniah 2:2. It was used twice concerning Jesus' death, once by Jesus Himself in Matthew 8:29, and once by Paul in Romans 5:6. It is found repeatedly in the Old Testament concerning the prescribed Jewish feasts that must be observed on set days. The four angels of the sixth trumpet judgment "had been prepared for the hour and day and month and year" (Rev. 9:15). Peter said, regarding Jesus' Second Coming, "He must remain in heaven until the time comes for God to restore everything, as he promised long ago through his holy prophets" (Acts 3:20-21 NIV).

THE APPOINTED TIME IN HOSEA

There is a prophecy in Hosea from which I believe we may learn the appointed time for the Millennium. And if we know when the Millennium will begin, we can also calculate the times of the events of the Seventieth Week of Daniel.

In this chapter, we will tell you when we believe Hosea's prophecy began, and why we are now close to the fulfillment of a major provision of that prophecy. If this is the correct interpretation, then why aren't we hearing more about it? Personally, I have heard or read only two others who have set forth the interpretation we are sharing with you. The first occasion was years ago when I was still a strong proponent of the pre-tribulation theory, at which time I dismissed the idea for the same reasons many will question this teaching. The second time was within the last five years, but neither source really developed the theory beyond a brief mention. Perhaps the reason why this is not being debated is that it is an indirect refutation of the doctrine of the imminent return of Christ.

Not many people, especially the unsaved, have the ability to recognize prophesied events that are being fulfilled right in front of them. For example, the Old Testament has dozens of prophecies concerning the birth of Jesus, His youth, ministry, death and resurrection. You can find a list of these fulfilled prophecies in several reference works.[34] Still, not many people living at the time of His birth actually made the connection between the prophecies and the drama that was unfolding around them. As Bible observers, we benefit from the proverbial 20/20 hindsight to find these numerous, but sometimes vague, predictions.

We are in the last years of this present age, and as the things we are studying materialize, God will enlighten the minds of those who are searching for them and enable them to share that knowledge with many. This is what Daniel said would happen, and what Paul confirmed to the Thessalonian church (Dan. 11:33-35; 12:3; 1 Thess. 5:20-21).

I am firmly convinced that this prophecy in Hosea gives us the time of the coming Kingdom. You have probably never heard it preached from the pulpit, and if you are able to find a commentary on this passage, it will probably say that it is an allegory, at most. Because it makes reference to "two days" and "third day," some commentators, almost as a reflex action, associate it with Jesus' death and resurrection instead of considering that it might be a major prophecy for God's chosen people and the start of "the age to come."

THE PROPHET

Hosea was a contemporary of Isaiah, and like him, a prophet to the ten northern tribes of Israel just before they were overrun by the Assyrians in 722 BC. His counterpart to the southern tribes a hundred years later was Jeremiah, who warned Judah about their impending captivity by the Babylonians in 606 BC. Both men were uniquely ordained to deliver warnings to a rebellious people.

You may recall that God told Hosea to marry a harlot and have "children of prostitution" (evidently they were not his own), to whom he was to give names that were significant to the message he was to deliver. His personal life was an object lesson not only of God's hatred of the people's idolatry, but also His love for them and His desire to restore them to fellowship.

"Israel" and "Judah"

When I read through the Bible as a youth, I was confused by the several uses of the name Israel. Israel means "strives with God," and was the name given to Jacob after he lost a prolonged wrestling match with the angel of the Lord. After his death, his twelve sons and their families were collectively called "the children of Israel" or just "Israel." When the kingdom split and ten tribes settled in the northern part of the country, they were also called Israel. Most recently, the modern nation of Israel was established by decree of the United Nations in 1948. As you read the Bible you must know whether the name is referring to the man, the people, the kingdom, the ten tribes, or the nation.

Meanwhile, the southern kingdom was referred to as Judah, after one of the two tribes that constituted that kingdom. The land they lived on was sometimes called Judea and the whole system of laws and tradition is known as Judaism.

It gets more complicated. Hosea also often addressed the ten northern tribes as Ephraim, the name of the tribe that bordered Judah. Since he lived among the northern tribes, it is not surprising when his prophecies are directed to them, but the prophecy under consideration was meant for all of the Israelites, including the southern kingdom of Judah. When Hosea had a prophecy for the whole nation, he would make a statement regarding his people (Ephraim or Israel) and lay along side it a similar statement concerning Judah, as in the example to follow.

> Therefore I am like a moth to Ephraim,
> And like rottenness to the house of Judah.
> When Ephraim saw his sickness,
> And Judah his wound.
> (Hosea 5:12-13a). [see also verses 5, 10, and 14.]

In the same manner that some people consider Hosea's prophecy a message only for the northern kingdom, so people also incorrectly infer that Jeremiah prophesied exclusively to the southern kingdom. To the contrary, the focus of this prophecy is not about the captivity of Ephraim, nor is Jeremiah's prophecy only about the Babylonian exile. Their prophecies concern a major act of God that affects all of Judaism. This was vividly brought to the attention of Ezekiel as he was told to take two sticks representing Ephraim and Judah and he then saw them being bonded into one (Ezek. 37:15ff).

THE PROPHECY

The heart of Hosea's prophecy follows. Because of an unfortunate assignment of verses by those who did such things, it spans a division of chapters and a casual reader may not connect the thoughts. First, Hosea speaks the mind of God regarding His punishment of Israel, and then he expresses the response of the people to the predicted punishment.

> For I will be like a lion to Ephraim, [the northern Kingdom]
> And like a young lion to the house of Judah. [the southern Kingdom]
> I, even I, will tear to pieces and go away,
> I will carry away, and there will be none to deliver.
> I will go away and return to My place

Until they acknowledge their guilt and seek My face;
In their affliction they will earnestly seek Me (Hosea 5:14-15).

Come, let us return to the Lord.
For He has torn us, but He will heal us;
He has wounded us, but He will bandage us.
He will revive us after two days;
He will raise us up on the third day
That we may live before Him (Hosea 6:1-2).

Lions are mentioned 110 times in the Old Testament. Some of the Bible characters, such as David and Sampson, had personal encounters with them. A lion will tear his prey apart, eat until satiated, and leave the remains for other predators. Hosea's audience knew precisely what God was telling them about their future, that after being severely punished, He would abandon them until such time that they would come to an end of themselves and turn back to Him. This theme is found in other prophecies by other prophets (Jer. 16:5-13; 17-18; 32:37-42; Ezek. 11:16; Mic. 5:8; Ps. 50:22).

When Israel returns to Him in their affliction at the end of the age, He will not only receive them, but He will also heal them and make provision for them to live with Him. We gave you references to the punishment above; compare them with His promises of restoration (Isa. 11:11-12; Jer. 16:14-15; 31:8-10; Ezek. 11:17; Mic. 4:6; and Zech. 2:6; 10:6).

A similar prophecy concerning both Israel and Judah was given to Jeremiah more than 100 years later, including the promise that they would be restored. The Jeremiah prophecy is interesting in that the northern kingdom had already been scattered all over the world. Those ten tribes have become so integrated into the societies of those countries that they are commonly referred to as "the ten lost tribes of Israel." In the end time, God will identify them and bring them back to himself.

The idea that Hosea and Jeremiah were speaking of the same punishment and restoration is compelling. Jeremiah wrote:

"For, behold, days are coming," declares the Lord, "when I will restore the fortunes of My people Israel and Judah." The Lord says, "I will also bring them back to the land that I gave to their forefathers, and they shall possess it."

"...All your lovers have forgotten you, they do not seek you; for I have wounded you with the wound of an enemy, with the punishment of a cruel one, because your iniquity is great and your sins are numerous....For I will restore you to health and I will heal you of your wounds," declares the Lord, "Because they have called you an outcast, saying: 'It is Zion; no one cares for her'" (Jer. 30:3, 14, 17). [See also Isa. 30:26; 60:10; Ezek. 20:33-38; 39:23-29.]

Fulfillment of the Prophecy

What makes the Hosea prophecy unique among similar prophecies is that it assigns times to both the abandonment and the restoration. Only Hosea 6:2 tells us that the punishment will last for "two days," after which they will live before Him on the "third day." Are these literal twenty-four hour days? Can we identify them in history or know what they will be in the future?

The precedent in the Bible for a "day" to represent a thousand years is found in the verses quoted below, one from the Old Testament and one from the New Testament. Dispensationalists use the same day/year principle in their interpretation that the seven days of creation is a type for the seven thousand year history of the earth, with the seventh, the day of rest, being the Millennium. In their theory, the earth was created 4,000 years before Jesus came the first time, and that we are now living in the last days of the sixth millennium.

But do not let this one fact escape your notice, beloved, that with the Lord one day is as a thousand years, and a thousand years as one day (2 Pet. 3:8).

For a thousand years in Thy sight
Are like yesterday when it passes by,
Or as a watch in the night (Ps. 90:4).

It may be easier for us to identify the "third day" in the Scriptures than the first "two days." All the teaching about the future Jewish Kingdom is that it is "everlasting," and it "has no end." But in the Revelation, we learn that the first thousand years of the Kingdom is a special time in God's plan. We call that period the "Millennium," which comes from the Latin words meaning "thousand years." That phrase is found six times in Revelation 20:2-7.

We know from the Bible that the Jews who are scattered around the world (the *Diaspora*) will be called back to a land especially prepared for them, where they will receive special blessings and closeness with the Messiah King. We believe that the Millennium will be the "third day" of Hosea's prophecy, and if it is, then the other two "days" must also each be one thousand years long. Therefore, we expect to see 2,000 years elapse between the "injury" to Israel and the beginning of the Millennium.

There is no evidence that the Millennium (the third day) has come, so we may or may not be living in the "two days." If we are *not* in that 2,000-year period, we should be looking for a coming event when God will "injure" Israel and "tear them in pieces." If we *are* in the 2,000 years, we should be able to identify such a significant event in the past and calculate the terminus of the "two days" in the future.

Injuries to Israel

There have been a number of "injuries" to Israel since Hosea wrote in the 8th century BC, some being more severe than others. The first was the captivity of the northern tribes by Assyria, when most of the Jewish population was scattered throughout the world. One hundred seventeen years later, the southern tribes, just two of the twelve, were taken to exile in Babylon.

One significant result of that conquest was that the beloved temple of Solomon was destroyed, although it was rebuilt after the Captivity. Four hundred years after the first temple was torn down, Antiochus IV (Epiphanes) desecrated the second temple by offering a pig sacrifice on the altar.[35] One hundred fifty years later, and just fifteen years before the birth of Jesus, King Herod began extensive renovations and additions to the temple complex. In AD 70, the Romans burned and leveled Herod's Temple, sold tens of thousands of Jews into slavery and dispersed most of the remainder throughout the world in what is known as the *Diaspora.* Another significant injury to the Jews was the crushing defeat of the Jewish zealots in the uprising of Bar-Kokhba in AD 132 to AD 135, with the resulting slaughter of 580,000 Jews and the destruction of 985 Jewish villages.[36] The Romans constructed a pagan temple on the site of the Jewish temple in an attempt to eradicate Judaism. They also changed the name of the land to Palestine, as it is to this day.

We could include the Spanish Inquisition and the Holocaust of less than seventy-five years ago in our list of assaults upon God's chosen people. The latter was the worse by far, in terms of human life, with six million Jews killed by Hitler's regime.

When attempting to identify the event of which Hosea wrote, we repeat the fact that, of all these disasters, *only* the destruction of Herod's Temple and the city of Jerusalem were mentioned in the prophecy of the seventy weeks of Daniel.

If Hosea's prophecy truly predicts a two thousand year separation from God after He "injured" them, then none of the incidents that occurred before the temple destruction could be the fulfillment of the prophecy, because they happened *more* than two thousand years ago. If any one of them was the intended fulfillment, we should be in the Millennium right now.[37]

But if the predicted injury to Israel is a disaster that came upon the Jews *after* the destruction of the temple, or if it is some unforeseen event in the future, then the Millennium is that much further off.

It should be obvious that I believe that the destruction of Jerusalem and the temple was the fulfillment of Hosea's prophecy of an injury to Israel. Dr. Chaim Weizmann, the first president of modern Israel, said in 1948,

"Jerusalem is the eternal mother of the Jewish people, precious and beloved even in its desolation. When David made Jerusalem the capital of Judea, on that day there began the Jewish

Commonwealth. When Titus destroyed it on the 9th of Ab, on that day there ended the Jewish Commonwealth."[38]

Note that this address was made *after* the Holocaust. It appears that Dr. Weizmann placed more significance to national Israel on the destruction of the city in AD 70 than to the murder of six million Jews by the Nazi regime.

It has been almost 2,000 years since the destruction of the temple, and the Kingdom could be nearly upon us. If it is, then we should want to know that. By calculating the end of the period in the same manner that Sir Robert Anderson calculated the date of the entry of Jesus into Jerusalem, we should be able to determine the start of the Kingdom.[39] Then, by interpreting Daniel's prophecies intelligently, we might also determine the dates for the covenant, the Abomination, the Rapture, and the Second Coming. They are God's Appointed Times.

The Time of the Millennium

There is no disputing the fact that Herod's temple was destroyed on the ninth day of the month Av in AD 70. The reason we mix the Jewish month with the Roman year is that the correct year by the Julian calendar is unquestionable. Likewise, the day and month are precisely known, because the Jews observe the event as *Tisha B'Av* every year in mourning.[40] According to Professor Alan D. Corre of the University of Milwaukee, the Julian day corresponding to the 9th Av in AD 70 was August 2.[41]

Now here is my speculation for your consideration. Daniel's prophecy of the seventy weeks of years was based upon a 360-day year. If we hold to that precedent for this prophecy, then our goal is to calculate the completion of 720,000 sunrises and sunsets. To get an accurate count, we have to first find the number of days from August 2, 0070 until October 4, 1582 (the Julian calendar), and add to that the number of days from October 15, 1582 (the Gregorian calendar) until the 720,000th day, including leap year's.[42]

The ten days skipped from October 4 to 15 were purposely eliminated by Pope Gregory's mathematicians to compensate for an error in the Julian calendar that observed a leap year every four years. The more accurate Gregorian calendar has an exception to the "every four years" rule. It only counts years ending in "00" and divisible by 400 as a leap year. Therefore, 1600 and 2000 were leap years, but 1700, 1800, and 1900 were not.

Using this information (or lack thereof) and the assumptions stated above and listed below, I have calculated that the Millennium will begin in November, 2041. Counting backwards 2,520 days says that the covenant will be signed in December 2034 or January, 2035 and that the Rapture will take place in September, 2041. There are enough uncertainties in the calendar and man's manipulation of those documents that we hesitate in presenting exact dates. Our precautions are listed below. The purpose of presenting this to you is not to be sensational or dramatic, but to have you think about this very important subject in the light of the Word and instruction from the Holy Spirit. The question for us all is, "How will you use the time between now and then?"

Can We Know the Time?
Many thousands of our brothers and sisters in Christ hold a view that is a virtual polar opposite of these conclusions. The uncertain time of return of Jesus has persuaded many of the hesitant or indifferent to put their trust in Jesus, and you can count the author among that number. It is difficult to deny that God has sanctioned the teaching of an imminent coming of Christ as an evangelical tool, and up to the present time, it did not matter what a person believed about the Rapture, because those people would die before the Rapture would take place. However, since the present generation (born after 1948?) will see these prophecies come to pass, they will have vital decisions to make and testimonies to uphold as we approach those times.

We have already set a tentative time for several eschatological events in this book, including the Rapture of the church, and by doing so, have challenged the theory of the imminent (at any moment) return of Jesus. We side-stepped this subject in the most natural place to discuss it, when we examined the Olivet discourse, where Jesus plainly spoke of His coming:

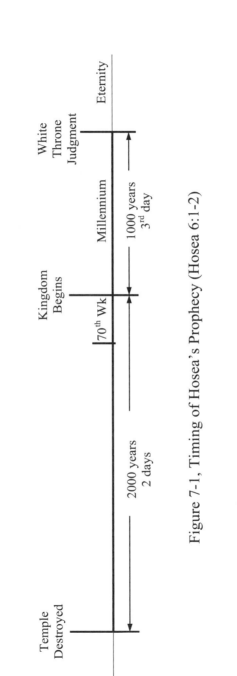

Figure 7-1, Timing of Hosea's Prophecy (Hosea 6:1-2)

But of that day and hour no one knows, not even the angels of heaven, nor the Son, but the Father alone. For the coming of the Son of Man will be just like the days of Noah. For as in those days which were before the flood they were eating and drinking, they were marrying and giving in marriage, until the day that Noah entered the ark, and they did not understand until the flood came and took them all away; so shall the coming of the Son of Man be (Matt. 24:36-39).

The fact that Jesus did not know the time of His own coming tells us that He did not have the attributes of God (such as omniscience) while He was in His flesh. The spiritual insight and knowledge He often showed came to Him either by special revelation from the Father or was included in the inspired writings for Him to learn. He knew the book of Hosea, but He did not know these forward-looking dates we have just discussed, *because the destruction of the temple had not yet happened.*

The verses above seem to be proof that we not only do not know when Jesus will return, but that we *cannot* know the time of His coming. Obviously, Jesus did not know the time of His return when He spoke these words, but is there any who would insist that He *still does not know* His Coming? The disciples once again asked Jesus about the times and seasons approximately forty days after His resurrection (Acts 1:6-7), and this time, He did not say that "no one knows the day," but that "it is not for *you* to know…." Stated differently, when Jesus returned to heaven after His resurrection, all the attributes of God, including omniscience, were conferred upon Him, and the statement He made in the Olivet discourse was no longer valid in all respects.

Likewise, Paul told the last generation believers that they would also know when the Day of the Lord was upon them (1Thess. 5:4-6). If you are alive when the covenant is signed, you know that Jesus will return in seven years. If you see on your television screen or on the Internet that a statue of a man claiming to be God is set up in the Jewish temple, you can confidently count out 1,260 days for the Resurrection and Rapture. If you live to the end of the Tribulation and see that the two witnesses were killed in the streets of Jerusalem, you would look for their resurrection in eighty-four hours (three and one-half days) and expect to be raptured immediately afterward.

Despite these clear statements of prophecy, it is also possible that some Christians will be just as surprised as the unsaved at His coming, since Jesus told the church at Sardis that they would miss His return if they didn't wake up to the obvious signs around them.

Return of the Jews to God

Two prophetic days, or 2,000 years after the destruction of Jerusalem and the temple, the Jews will return to God *en masse*, not just a boatload now and again or daily flights to Israel, but millions of them. Hosea 5:15 said that they will seek Him *in their affliction*, so we might recall what prophetic event or events will shake them from their present complacency. Actually, that is rather easy to identify, given that the seventieth week of Daniel immediately precedes the Millennium. The last half of the week includes both the Tribulation and the Day of the Lord; a period we believe is what Jeremiah called "The Time of Jacob's Trouble."

> For, lo, the days come, saith the Lord, that I will bring again the captivity of my people Israel and Judah, saith the Lord: and I will cause them to return to the land that I gave to their fathers, and they shall possess it.
>
> And these are the words that the Lord spake concerning Israel and concerning Judah. For thus saith the Lord; We have heard a voice of trembling, of fear, and not of peace. Ask ye now, and see whether a man doth travail with child? Wherefore do I see every man with his hands on his loins, as a woman in travail, and all faces are turned into paleness? Alas! for that day is great, so that none is like it: it is even the time of Jacob's trouble; but he shall be saved out of it (Jer. 30:3-7).

We have discussed the return of the Jews at greater length in the chapter The Day of the Lord. Although it is necessary that they will seek the Lord, it is also true that God will send others to search for them. They will gather in a desert place, where they will be judged by Him and the unworthy culled out. The remainder, only about one-third of their number, will be given a new heart and will enter the Promised Land.

It is with no small measure of trepidation that the above was written, not that I fear what any man or woman might say about putting a date on these events. I'm too old to care about that, and I have no dependence upon any organization for any compensation or censure. But neither do I want to grieve the Lord in any way. My conviction that this approach is basically right has only grown as I watch current events play out, confirming God's Word.

QUALIFIERS TO THE INTERPRETATION

While the last generation will accurately know the date of the coming of the Lord when they see the Abomination, we cannot know it with that same certainty. The comments I have made in this chapter are based upon several assumptions:

- The first assumption is that the passage in Hosea is indeed a prophecy for the end of the age and the beginning of the kingdom of God.
- The second is that the "days" of the Hosea passage are each one thousand years long.
- Third, that the years (as in the thousand years) are each 360 days long.
- Fourth, that the event that determined the beginning of the Hosea prophecy (the injury to Israel) was indeed the destruction of the temple and Jerusalem in AD 70.
- Fifth, although it is known that the temple destruction was on 9 Av in the civil year AD 70, was that date really the 2nd of August?

Regardless of what you may have heard, God is not waiting for the church to do something that will trigger the coming of Christ. Neither does something have to happen to Israel or Europe, nor some law passed, other than what the prophecies already tell us. God does nothing without first revealing it to His prophets (Amos 3:7). He has an appointed time for these things, and the fulfillment of this prophecy may be the indicator of what that time is.

In the second chapter, we discussed the final week of Daniel's prophecy, which ends when the Millennium, or the third "day" that Hosea wrote about, begins. Please see the time line in figure 7-1 for a visual presentation of the relationship of these events.

IMPLICATIONS FOR THE CONTEMPORARY CHRISTIAN

If the premise of this book is true, then we can know with some certainty when the Millennium will begin, and seven years before that time, we can look for the events of the seventieth week to start being fulfilled.

If the premise of this book is true, then we cannot say that Jesus will return at any moment. Paul said that the believer of the last generation would know when the Day of the Lord will come.

If the premise of this book is true, then you should teach it to your children and your children's children with more intensity as the time approaches. They, of all people, should not enter into the final seven years of this age without knowing the things that will come upon the church and Israel.

Jesus told the disciples that they should look for signs of the end-times just as diligently as they look to nature for clues that it is time to plant and reap. Allow me to suggest several trends and events that will take place before or early into the seventieth week. Some of these are speculation based upon trends in society, and some are certain facts we are told in the Bible.

- Increasing discrimination against anything pertaining to the God of the Bible, and especially against His Son, Jesus. This has begun as "separation of church and state," will be next exercised in the public arena, and will then work into privacy issues, that is, what you will be able to do in your home.

- More and more limitations of the rights of those who exalt the name and person of Jesus. Churches will lose their tax-exempt status, first on bookstores, daycare, etc. and then on real estate. Donors will have to pay taxes on contributions. Churches will be told what they can build, and where.
- Ten countries will form an alliance, or ten nations will evolve from an existing coalition to become a single entity, while retaining their identities.
- A strong charismatic man will wrest control of his country by stealth and intrigue in a time of peace. Supernatural events propel that man to world-class status.
- He will become the de facto leader of the ten-nation alliance after subduing three of them that oppose him.
- A push will be made for all countries to modify their laws and policies for the sake of "globalization," even to the point that they will grant control of their armed forces to a world body.

   Middle East tensions will again flare up, this time threatening Jerusalem. The UN or EU, or even the ten-nation alliance will draft a seven-year treaty that will result in an interim peace. Don't be surprised if a resolution, covenant, treaty, or peace agreement that does not quite meet the Bible's criteria is presented before the true one is signed.
- Preparations for the Jewish temple to be built on the Temple Mount.

If the premise of this book is true, then we should be mentally preparing to dispose of much of our personal assets. As we said earlier, the authority and influence of the Antichrist will probably not be uniformly onerous everywhere in the world. He may have absolute power in some countries of the Middle East and Europe, but less in the Pacific Islands, the Far East, or the United States. If you are sitting on a large savings account, stock portfolio, real estate, etc., and you see a powerful man rising in the pattern of the Antichrist, or a seven year treaty signed, or an abomination set up in the temple at Jerusalem, you know that those assets will be worthless at the end of the age. You should put their value into the hands of someone who is presenting the gospel and winning souls or caring for the body of Christ.

If the premise of this book is true, then every Christian should be purifying himself or herself by holy living and a sanctified life, seeking out and obeying every precept laid out in the Bible. God will not leave His people or His church defenseless under the influence of the Antichrist. There will be 144,000 undefiled, blameless Jews that will be preserved through the Tribulation and the Wrath of God who will be the "firstfruits" of a much larger number (Rev. 14:4-5). Likewise, there will be select Christians similarly preserved who meet the criteria of the Philadelphia church (Rev. 3:8, 10). To be counted among one of these groups will require ever-vigilant devotion and constant guard of one's daily walk. Unfortunately, not many will follow this advice and will find their faith severely tested, even to the death.

WITNESSING FAITH

We have been studying a large number of prophecies in this book, both from an expository and topical approach, and we have seen how they all may fit together. Christians are people of faith, but to the unbeliever, the faith that we place in unfulfilled prophecy imparts virtually no weight to the arguments that we might present to them. Demonstrable fulfillment of prophecy, on the other hand, is tangible proof of the reality of our faith. If the first portions of prophecy have been fulfilled as predicted, then by extension, the balance of the prophecy may be confidently anticipated; and the more prophecies that we can document as having literally come to pass, the more confidence we have that the remainder will be literally fulfilled as well. Sir Robert Anderson said it better, "Unfulfilled prophecy is only for the believer, but prophecy fulfilled has a voice for all." [43]

A Primer of Bible Prophecy

Secular prophecy has been exploited by many who wish to profit (pun intended) from the interest the subject generates in a host of people. The tabloid magazines that are seemingly omnipresent in checkout lanes come to mind. At the start of each year, dozens of predictions are made regarding current issues and personalities, and the "prophet" in our midst is rewarded with book deals, syndicated columns, and television appearances if only one of them comes close to being fulfilled.

Sadly, similar things could be said of the religious among us. The Bible contains a wealth of prophecies that were meant for a particular people, place, and time. Many of them have already been fulfilled, but some people persist in finding new promises in them to apply to the church. A prophecy may be quite clear about its predictions, including answers to the questions of who, what, why, when, and where; but there are those who imagine fulfillments far beyond what the Bible record warrants. As a whole, we have not been diligent to judge contemporary false prophets, as God told us we should.

This appendix provides basic instruction for the beginning student of Bible prophecy so he or she can discern from the Scriptures what God is saying to His people. Hopefully they will also acquire a basis for detecting the errors that some deliver to the uninformed. We have examined specific prophecies in some detail in this book.

A word of caution to the reader may be in order. The cryptic and often vague language of prophecy sometimes leaves the interpretation of the fulfillment open to speculation, which in turn can develop into a competition to find a better (and often more bizarre) explanation than others have offered. Many good people have developed a consuming interest in things to come, to the neglect of other sound doctrines. The apostle Peter wisely instructed Christians to first be nourished with the basics of the faith, and later, to learn the deeper truths of the word, much as an infant requires milk for early development and solid foods when he has grown a little (1 Peter 2:2-3). The study of prophecy, to be useful to the Christian, first requires knowledge of the Word, and after that, thought, reason, and balance.

If you find yourself spending an inordinate amount of time pursuing speculative evidences of end-time events, you would do well to devote more time and effort toward achieving a balanced perspective of the whole counsel of God, whether it is related to doctrine, church life, evangelism, etc. The operative word here is "speculative," as the facts of prophecy may be learned in a relatively short time, while speculation can be never-ending.

DICTIONARY DEFINITIONS

It is always safe to start a study with a dictionary definition. The following is from Webster's New World Dictionary.

Prophesy (prof' uh sigh) v.t. 1. To declare or predict (something) by or as by the influence of divine guidance; utter (prophecies). 2. To predict (a future event) in any way. Example: "Isaiah began to *prophesy* regarding the coming Messiah."

Prophecy (prof' uh see) n. 1. Prediction of the future under the influence of divine guidance; act or practice of a prophet. 2. Any prediction. 3. Something prophesied or predicted. Example: "Students began to study the *prophecy* of Isaiah."

BIBLE DEFINITION

In the Old Testament, there are two Hebrew words that convey the meaning of a prophecy. One (*nbuwah*) is used three times to clearly refer to predictions and is translated "prophecy." It comes from the root word (*nabi*) meaning speaker or spokesman, found some 288 times in the Old Testament as a noun and 102 times in verb form. The other (*massa)* is used for a literal or figurative load to carry, or a prophetic utterance (25 times), most often translated "burden" in the KJV and "oracle" in the NIV and NASB. The root word (*nasa*) means "to lift."

The New Testament Greek word is *propheteia* (19 times). It comes from *propheteuo* (28 times), which derives from *prophetes* (144 times) meaning "interpreter" or "forth-teller of the divine will."

Some churches call their ministers prophets, not because they tell the future, but because their message reflects God's will for the congregation. Most people today associate prophecy with prediction and fulfillment, and that is the element of prophecy that we use in this book.

THE PURPOSES OF PROPHECY

Unfulfilled predictions of an untested prophet mean little. I could predict the invention of an engine that will use water as a fuel, and technically I will not be wrong if I do not attach a deadline for the fulfillment. If the machine is developed a thousand years from now, I will have been right and should have my portrait in some hall of fame. If no one invents such a machine, the prophecy remains in the category of "unfulfilled" and I continue to be an obscure nobody.

Likewise, there is no value in a trivial statement such as "The sun will rise tomorrow."

The primary purpose of *fulfilled* prophecy is the *verification of God's Word.* When the prophet of God speaks a word for the future and it comes to pass, the observer will presumably accept the divine nature of the oracle, and thus, the Word.

A second purpose for fulfilled prophecy is for the *validation of the prophet.* Having demonstrated that what he says comes to pass, those who hear him are disposed to believe other things he may say. The Bible sets a high standard for a prophet. *He or she must be 100 percent accurate.* In times past, the penalty for speaking on behalf of God and having your words fail was to be stoned to death. Modern "prophets" who have erred in their prophecy are fortunate because society frowns upon our stoning of them. Unfortunately for the church, followers of a charismatic leader tend to be more loyal to him than to his message, and overlook the fact that they are sometimes, perhaps often, wrong.

Third, Bible prophecy was sometimes given so that there would be *changed behavior* on the part of those to whom the prophecy is directed. In the case of conditional prophecy (see below), the desired response might delay or cancel the prophecy. This is not unlike the warning that a child might receive from a parent, either to prevent injury in a dangerous situation, or to avoid punishment for his disobedience.

Fourth, God *communicates His plans* for His people through His spokesmen before He acts upon them.

> Surely the Lord God does nothing unless He reveals His secret counsel to His servants the prophets (Amos 3:7).

We can be assured that what God is going to do in the future, He has already told us. If there is more to be revealed, He will do it through prophets, and the fulfillment of their oracles will be the authenticating sign that they are true prophets.

PROPHETIC BIBLE PASSAGES

We are told that as much as one-third of the Bible is prophecy, if we include the original prophecies, any interpretations, and the fulfillments. Thirty-three percent of the Word testifies to the importance that God places on prophecy. Paul said, "Prophecy is for a sign, not to unbelievers, but to those who believe" (1 Cor. 14:22). Prophecy is not intended to be a soul-winning tool, although it has been used effectively as such. Its primary purpose is to inform and build up the body of Christ.

Almost every book of the Bible contains some prophecy, but a few contain enough to be categorized as a prophetic book, as are the books of Isaiah through Malachi in the Old Testament and Revelation in the New Testament. Other books contain significant prophetic passages, such as the book of Psalms, the gospels, and the epistles.

Much of Old Testament prophecy was directed to Israel, with warnings couched in prophecies that were conditional regarding their attitude toward God. They were promised blessings if they would shun idolatry and not mistreat their fellow Jew. If they were disobedient, then God would punish them severely, even to the point that He would allow their enemies to conquer them. A good number of "burdens" or oracles are directed to the enemies of Israel who were taking advantage of Israel's diminished numbers and weakened defenses.

The Old Testament contains books labeled "Major Prophets" and "Minor Prophets," based primarily upon how lengthy they are. The larger books, such as Isaiah, Jeremiah, and Ezekiel contain both prophecies that have been fulfilled, and unfulfilled prophecies that complement the eschatology of Daniel with details of the Day of the Lord, the return of exiled Jews, and the coming messianic Kingdom. In the Gospels, the Olivet discourse of Jesus recorded in Matthew, Mark, and Luke concerns the end times. The "resurrection chapter" of 1 Corinthians 15 is closely associated with the Rapture. Parts of 1 Thessalonians 4-5 and 2 Thessalonians 2 are keys to an understanding of major events of the end times. People read the Revelation for things not found anywhere else, yet the Revelation is continually referring to Old Testament types. These are passages you will want to understand thoroughly.

ESCHATOLOGY

A special study of Bible prophecy is *Eschatology* (es' ka tol' ə-ji), which pertains solely to end-time events. This is unfulfilled prophecy by definition, but I believe that there are many reading this that will see these prophecies fulfilled in their lifetimes. They should be *especially* interested in what the prophecies say and when they might come to pass. But as we said in the opening paragraphs, some pastors today studiously avoid the subject of eschatology except for the occasional "Jesus may come at any moment" warning. Part of the reason they are reluctant to teach it is a fear that some of their people will become fixated on the subject, but it may also be their own lack of a comprehensive understanding of the events. A balance is needed in the teaching and preaching of this subject, especially since we are now likely instructing the last generation that will experience "all these things."

CONDITIONAL VS. UNCONDITIONAL PROPHECY

All eschatology that I am aware of is *unconditional,* that is, it will take place exactly as predicted, regardless of anything we do. The Bible tells us that even Satan will try to change "times and laws" (Dan. 7:25), but he will fail. However, there are things that individuals can do to avoid the *consequences* of some prophecies. Anyone who believes that Jesus is the Son of God and died for our sins will be granted exemption from eternal punishment. The righteous Jew (the 144,000) and Christian (the Philadelphia church) are promised protection in tribulation.

Not only will end-time prophecies be fulfilled regardless of anything we may do, but they will also come at precise times already determined by God. It is revealing to study the number of times in the Bible where "the appointed time" or "in the fullness of time" or some similar phrase occurs. There is no uncertainty with God's plans.

There are also *conditional* prophecies in the Bible. These usually predict a dire circumstance that will come about unless some person, group, or nation responds in the way God requires. A well-known conditional prophecy was Jonah's prophesied destruction of the city of Nineveh (Jonah 3:4-10). The whole city, including the officials, immediately repented and the destruction was avoided (much to Jonah's disappointment). You may also recall that God said that He would bless His people, Israel, if they followed His commandments, but that disasters, such as crop failure or defeat in battle, would come upon them if they did not. The same principle is true for all who worship God.

TIMING OF FULFILLED PROPHECY

Some prophecies had a short-term (even immediate) fulfillment, while others have not been fulfilled after thousands of years. Some, like the seventy weeks of Daniel, have been assigned a definite length of time, while others are open-ended. Jonah's prophecy to Nineveh, mentioned above, was to be fulfilled within forty days of the announcement (Jonah 3:4). To the other extreme, the prophecy to Eve in the Garden of Eden regarding her seed bruising the head of the serpent will not be fulfilled until the Day of the Lord (Gen. 3:15).

Unfortunately, it is fairly common for some to appropriate promises or prophecies intended for a specific people and time, and apply it to the church or to a personal situation in which they are involved. They may be piously expecting the completion of a prophecy that has already been fulfilled, and in that respect, is "dead." People can be greatly disillusioned when they don't receive the answer they sincerely thought God promised them, even to the point that they turn from the faith.

For example, take these following words that God spoke to Solomon regarding Israel. It is based upon the premise that God had ordained punishment upon a sinful people, but that He would restore them to fellowship if they repent.

> If I shut up the heavens so that there is no rain, or if I command the locust to devour the land, or if I send pestilence among My people, and My people who are called by My name humble themselves and pray, and seek My face and turn from their wicked ways, then I will hear from heaven, will forgive their sin, and will heal their land (2 Chron. 7:13-14).

The principle of this promise is certain, that God will respond favorably to the fervent prayers of His people. However, the passage above said that He would forgive and heal in those instances where He was inflicting punishment for disobedience. Most people do not quote the first half of the verse. We have to recognize that there are times when God allows hardship, not as a form of punishment, but rather to strengthen or to educate His people. Haven't you gone through a particularly stressful situation and found yourself closer to the Lord and more intense in your prayers because of it? Or have you come through a figurative valley, only to realize that He was guiding you toward a particular end result? We have every right to petition God for relief, but He is not obligated to answer on the basis of the above promise.

PROPHECIES WITH DUAL FULFILLMENT

There are prophecies that are written in such a way that the reader would expect to see all the details fulfilled at one time, only to realize that the fulfillment differs from the prophecy in some detail. The prophecy has not failed; it is only that the rest of the fulfillment is coming at another time. The prophecy of Daniel chapter eight was partially realized in an historic king (Antiochus IV), but some details have not been fulfilled. Daniel was told that the complete fulfillment would come in the end time.

"Dual fulfillment" has been illustrated as a person looking at distant objects that are in visual alignment, like a building on one hill and a tower on another. To the observer, they appear to be together, while in fact they are widely separated.

PROGRESSIVE PROPHECY

The first time a prophecy is delivered, it is often lacking in detail. For example, the seventieth week of Daniel, the Antichrist, and the Abomination are all mentioned in just one short verse (Dan. 9:27). Daniel was told more about the Antichrist in chapter 11, and about the thirty-day and forty-five-day periods in chapter 12. Much later, Jesus put His coming in perspective relative to the Abomination and the Tribulation in the Olivet discourse (Matt. 24-25). Paul gave us understanding of the Resurrection and the Rapture in 1 Corinthians 15, again in 1 Thessalonians 4 and 5, and also in 2 Thessalonians 2 (including the Day of the Lord). Finally we have the detail of the Revelation, recorded by John. This is called *progressive prophecy*, where later prophecies shed more light on subject material that had been revealed earlier.

It is important to know that none of the latter passages contradict the former, but add to it. Taken together, all the prophecies give us a far better picture of what will take place in the end times. But because they were often given hundreds of years apart and by different men in different settings, the tendency is to treat them as separate events, especially if details in the earlier passages are not repeated in the latter, or are stated differently.

If you suspect that two prophets are describing the same event, you need to examine the facts of both prophecies to see if they are consistent. If they appear to be inconsistent, you must consider that it is probable that it is your understanding of them that needs to change, not that they are deficient. It is human nature to misunderstand a teaching if it conflicts with what you were previously told. It may be true that the prophets are talking of two different things entirely. This is where we are especially dependent upon the Holy Spirit to teach us.

HOW PROPHETS RECEIVED PROPHECY

I have always been wary of those who feel compelled to publicly announce what God has "given" to them, especially if it is a departure from God's Word or radically new. It is one thing to have a moving experience in a time of devotion or during a moving church service, or waking in the middle of the night with a strong thought in mind, but it is quite another to experience the visions or revelations that prophets in the Bible had, or to be released by the Holy Spirit to make those visions public. Some people are quite taken with the "prophecies" or "predictions" of Nostradamus or Jean Dixon, but we should be reminded that the Bible criterion for a true prophet is complete accuracy when they speak for God. We should have "zero tolerance" for self-proclaimed prophets who are proven to be false. If they predict one thing that is contrary to the Bible, or if one prophecy is found to be wrong, we must pay no more attention to them and stop supporting them in any way.

It is interesting to see how prophets received and delivered their messages. Forty-nine times, Ezekiel said "the word of the Lord came unto me," but he doesn't say *how* it came to him. Some prophets had *dreams,* but while we often cannot remember our dreams when we wake up, the prophets remembered theirs in vivid detail.

A good number of prophecies came in the form of *visions.* For a long time, I struggled for the distinction between a vision and a dream, until I came across the Bible definition: "The oracle of him who hears the words of God, who sees the vision of the Almighty, falling down [the KJV reads 'trance'], yet having his eyes uncovered," (Num. 24:4). I have to confess that I can only imagine what that is like. Did the prophet see it as though it was projected on a screen, or did he find himself in the middle of the action? Isaiah often said, "I saw," and makes it clear that he actually witnessed the things he related. The same could be said of John regarding the Revelation, when he was carried to heaven in the Spirit.

Some prophecies were *spoken* directly to the prophet by a messenger, face-to-face like you talk to a friend. In the case of Daniel, the angel Gabriel was named as the messenger. "The Revelation of Jesus Christ" was delivered to John by an angel sent by Jesus. God Himself spoke directly to Moses.

The message of the book of Haggai is unusual, in that the word of the Lord came both to the prophet, Haggai, and to the high priest, Joshua. We are not told whether they received the message when they were together, or if they were given it separately and later compared experiences.

A very few prophecies were received in *writing.* The first copy of the Ten Commandments was written by the finger of God (but Moses destroyed it in anger). The scroll John saw in heaven, the one sealed with seven seals, was pre-written. Both Ezekiel and John were given a book (scroll) to eat because they were to prophesy regarding the contents at a later time.

HOW THE PROPHETS DELIVERED PROPHECY

Because we have Bible prophecy *in writing,* we tend to think that they were first delivered that way, and some of them were. At one time, Jeremiah was told to have a scribe record everything God had given him, from the first to the last (Jer. 36: 1-32). This account was read to the people in the temple and they repented, but when the book was read to the king, he burned it. God told Jeremiah to rewrite it, with added material. Perhaps this is the book of Jeremiah we now have in our Bibles. Jeremiah also wrote to the exiles in Babylon (Jer. 29:1-28) when he couldn't go there personally.

Many of the prophecies were first *spoken* to the audience by inspiration, and written down by a scribe later for preservation.

Isaiah, Jeremiah, and Ezekiel were told to do some weird things as *object lessons* to get the message across. How long would you keep your preacher if one day he shaved his head, stuffed a few hairs into his pocket, chopped up one-third, scattered one-third to the winds, and burned one-third in front of the congregation? This is what Ezekiel did in obedience to God (Ezek. 5:1-4). Would you hire a pastor who included in his resume the fact that he bought a belt, wore it a while, then buried it down by the river, only to retrieve it later? Anyone who thinks that the prophets and prophecy are boring should review these stories.

Allow me one last vital thought about the Bible in general, and prophecy in particular. The Bible was written by a number of men of diverse cultures, languages, and locations over a very long span of time, and yet they agree on the message that God has for us, even without knowing what was previously written. The Bible is a miraculous book, unique in its truthfulness and endurance. Christians are people of faith, but we do not have a groundless faith.

Scientists continually seek the secrets of the universe, but they still disagree on the theories they propose and often have to revise them when their experiments with ever more sophisticated tools reveal their original errors. Historians are continually revising explanations of our past, due in part to the discoveries of archaeologists, which is honorable, but also to be "politically correct," to their shame. We cannot rely on these "experts" for long, while the Bible remains rock solid.

Likewise, God has been revealing the details of the end of the age through His prophets and better understanding of His word. He showed Daniel a vision and said that it pertains to the end-time. John was told that he was not to write down some of the revelation he saw, saying that it would be revealed at the appropriate time. Daniel learned that when it was time, certain people would be taught these truths and share them with others. The proper understanding of prophecy leads us to acknowledge a God who is infinitely wiser than we are and obediently follow the truth as it is revealed to us.

Appendix B

Interpretation of Scripture

As a conscientious student, you want to understand fully what the Holy Spirit had to say through the authors of the Bible when they wrote. These scribes thought in languages other than ours and lived in cultures that were very much different, over a span of hundreds of years. They lived in places you and I have never seen, and chances are that even if you were to go there today, they would not look the same as they did then. Archeologists often dig through many feet of dirt and debris to get to the sites as they were when the Bible was written.

I don't believe that we could ever have a full appreciation of the work of those who have translated God's Word into languages other than the original Greek, Hebrew, or Aramaic. However, the meaning of the words the prophets and translators used may have changed over time. (What did "gay" mean to your grandparents?) For a number of years I worked for a British company and have had many interesting and sometimes humorous discussions with my counterparts from "across the pond," comparing the diverse meanings of the same words in our respective cultures.

How can we process the ideas that God gave to the prophets and "get it right" every time? If you have listened to a number of sermons, you know that not everyone has the same interpretations of any given passage. An observant person once said that, if you ask two students of prophecy a question, they will have three opinions.

The skeptics often say that, "anything can be proven from the Bible." Unfortunately, this is true if the one manipulating the Scripture is devious or careless in the use of the Bible. To prevent, or at least to mitigate, this practice, scholars have systematized a discipline called *Hermeneutics*, which is sometimes defined as *the art and science of Bible interpretation*. It is a science inasmuch as the practitioner must identify and adopt rules that are to be rigidly followed. It is an art because one must understand the mind of the Holy Spirit in the interpretation, which comes from familiarity with the Book and the Author.

But while sincere scholars seek a discipline to prevent the misuse of interpretation, strong differences of opinion remain, due in part to the *approach* that each brings to the study. Broad groupings of these approaches have led to what are called *Schools of Interpretation*. One school of interpretation may call itself *literal*, and say that the Bible should be read as meaning just what it says. The school that believes that the same things are *allegorical* read the words as symbolic and seeks for an application of what they mean. Ramm lists three divisions of the literal school, three more in the allegorical school, and three additional schools (devotional, liberal, and neo-orthodoxy).[44]

Just when you begin to feel comfortable with the school you have chosen, more decisions present themselves. If scholars view prophecy as not yet fulfilled, they might call themselves *futurists*. Others who believe that prophecy has been and is presently being fulfilled are proud *historists*. There is a third group called *preterists*, whose belief is that all prophecy was fulfilled prior to AD 70 and the destruction of the Jewish temple. And this is not where differences end.

Regardless of the school with which one may choose to identify, it is important that each is *consistent* with his or her personal interpretation. It is not unusual for a person to have a conclusion in mind even at the outset of a study. They may have had this inculcated in them by someone with whom they closely identify, or they may have a strong desire to show a particular outcome, but it is easy to switch "schools" when trying to preserve an idea. I have witnessed a number of people who claim to believe in literal fulfillment of prophecy suddenly allegorize a passage when the literal interpretation is not supportive of their position.

This book uses a literal, futurist approach to the study of prophecy. Having said that, even a literalist deserves to be given the latitude of recognizing the various literary methods for what they are: similes, metaphors, symbols, etc. These are means by which descriptive terms illustrate real things. For example, all sports teams adopt a mascot as their icon. No one reading the sports section of a newspaper would assume that the Miami Dolphins were actually aquatic mammals playing football. Likewise, a beast in Scripture, said to have seven heads and ten horns, is also a representation of something tangible that we must identify to properly understand the prophecy.

INTERPRETIVE HELPS

There are reference works that Bible students should obtain for their library. They are available in many bookstores, or they may found on the Internet. A person familiar with a computer should take advantage of the several excellent Bible software programs that have various versions of the Bible, concordances, atlases, commentaries, and dictionaries that can be used to create one's own documents. Other suggested helps unique to Bible interpretation are:

- Bible dictionary
- Bible atlas
- Translations of the Bible
- An exhaustive concordance
- Old and New Testament Surveys
  (A summary of prophets, kings, and major events in their time sequence
- Books on the manners and customs of the Bible
- A book on Hermeneutics (review annually)

THINGS TO ASK REGARDING A PASSAGE

With all of this background, it is still extremely important that one read the Bible with an understanding of what it actually says. It is inevitable that we each integrate our base of knowledge into what we read in the Bible, to some degree and often subconsciously. When a citizen of a modern, western culture sees the word, "house," he tends to think of frame construction, shingled roof, and glass windows; rather than the thick stone walls, thatched roof, open windows, an open fireplace, water gathered in pots, and crude toilets of an early biblical village. A road in the times of the Bible was basically a wide path, and twenty miles was a day's walk in homemade sandals. When one has been taught a particular interpretation from an early age, it is difficult to accept the truth of another view, even when it is clearly scriptural.

Try to put yourself into the context of the author. Who wrote it? To whom was it written? Where and when was it written? In what language? What were the circumstances at the time it was written? What was the political climate? What season of the year was it? Was there prosperity or famine? What was the geography where he lived? What was the topology? What has changed since then?

It is also helpful to know how the authors of the Bible interrelate, where and when they lived and who the kings and priests were at the time. It is interesting that Jeremiah, Ezekiel, and Daniel all lived during the Babylonian Captivity and wrote from widely different perspectives. Daniel served in the palace among the highest officials in the land. Ezekiel ministered in the Jewish ghetto of Babylon, and Jeremiah wrote from Jerusalem or Egypt.

CONTEXT

Many errors of interpretation are made when the student does not pay attention to the *context* of prophecy. It is important that we take into consideration that which comes before and after a selected text, to evaluate what effect it has upon the prophecy. Look beyond the divisions of verses and chapters, which while helpful, sometimes are misleading. Beware of any expositor who skips verses, stops in the middle of a passage, or pulls "proof texts" from a number of passages without close examination A good scholar will chase down as many facts as he can that relate to his study, and he will not allow himself to ignore any fact just because it contradicts a conclusion he might otherwise reach.

OTHER SOURCES

Matthew, Mark, and Luke have written what we call the *synoptic* gospels. That is, they often wrote about the same events. But because of their different personalities, backgrounds, ages, etc., there are differences in their records. These differences often give us a more complete picture of Jesus' ministry. They do not often conflict, but complement each other.

CONCLUSION

Bible prophecy is a very complicated subject with hundreds of examples to study, both those that have been fulfilled and those for which we are waiting the revelation. But perhaps more important than just identifying the facts of prophecies, especially those pertaining to eschatology, is the method of interpreting those facts in a manner that is consistent with revealed truth in the Word of God and that which is going on around us. Perhaps the hardest tasks of all are to approach the Word with absolutely no biases and to handle the facts with total honesty. Oh yes, and to be able to say, when appropriate, "I don't know."

Notes

1. There was a series of minor kings that ruled Babylon after Nebuchadnezzar died and before Belshazzar began to reign, Evil-Merodach (two years), Neriglissar (three years), and Labashi-Marduk (two years). Belshazzar became a co-regent with his father, Nabonidus, in the first year of Belshazzar (Dan. 7:1). Three years later, Nabonidus went to handle affairs in Arabia, leaving Belshazzar as regent in Babylon in the third year of Belshazzar (Dan. 8:1). The Bible views the importance of these kings differently than does history.

2. The dates I use are those calculated in <u>The Coming Prince</u> by Sir Robert Anderson, 10th edition, 1957, Kregel Publications, Grand Rapids, Michigan, pp 122ff.

3. The Hebrew word used here is translated elsewhere in the Old Testament 312 times as "prophet." Only here is it translated "prophecy."

4. The evolution of the Jewish calendar is a fascinating study, developing from an observed study of the moons and seasons endorsed by the priesthood, to the present rigorous technical document.

5. Sir Robert Anderson, <u>The Coming Prince</u>, 10th edition, Kregel Publications, Grand Rapids, 1957, pg. 256.

6. There is a discrepancy between Anderson's calculations in the late 19th century and recent calendars. Some of this may be attributed to the way that the years are counted (transition from BC to AD) and some between the Julian and Gregorian calendars.

7. The Antichrist will reveal himself by "sitting in the temple of God, showing himself to be God" (2 Thess. 2:3-4). I believe that he will do this in the middle of the week, shortly before or coincident with his image being erected in the temple.

8. The involvement of the United Nations in middle-east peace negotiations has already been suggested.

9. "The Coming Last Days Temple," Randall Price, Harvest House Publishers, Eugene Washington, 1999, page 332.

10. "Secrets of Jerusalem's Temple Mount," Leen and Kathleen Ritmeyer, Biblical Archaeology Society, Washington D.C., 1998, page 86.

11. "The Coming Last Days Temple," Randall Price, Harvest House Publishers, Eugene Washington, 1999, page 342ff.

12. Webster's New World Dictionary, David B. Guralnik, General Editor, The World Publishing Company, Cleveland and New York.

13. Arutz Sheva, www.IsraelNationalNews.com.

14. www.JewishEncyclopedia.com, "Sandhedrin."

15. An abomination of the temple in the 2nd century BC resulted when the Greek ruler, Antiochus Epiphanes, erected an altar to Zeus in the Jewish temple and offered a sacrifice of a pig on that altar. He then boiled the pig's flesh and splashed the defiled broth on the sanctuary walls, floors, and furnishings. Jesus made it clear that the abomination of Antiochus was not the one that Daniel wrote about, which will come in the end-time (Matt. 24:15-16).

16. Some translations read that the number is the number of *a* man, that is, unique to him alone, and others say that it is the number of *man*, that is, symbolic of the secular world. [There is no indefinite article in the Greek; these are inserted at the discretion of the translator.] Regarding the latter, if you take the Roman numerals D = 500, C = 100, L = 50, X = 10, V = 5, and I = 1 and add them, DCLXVI = 666. The letter M, for 1000, was not used by the Romans at the time the Revelation was written.

17. When the celestial signs are related to the Coming of Jesus, they include the falling stars, but not with the Day of the Lord that immediately follows (Matt. 24:29; Rev. 6:13). The author believes that the "stars" falling to earth are the souls of dead saints that Jesus brings with Him,

who rise from the earth to receive transformed bodies and then rejoin
Jesus in the clouds with the raptured saints. See the book of the
Revelation for other examples of living beings called "stars."

18. The KJV translation of 2 Thessalonians 2:2 reads "day of Christ," but the
word *kurios* is used there and is more properly translated "Day of the
Lord" by the NIV, NASV, and others. See also 1 Corinthians 1:8, "Day of
our Lord Jesus."

19. There are two places on the Temple Mount where the original peaks
outcroppings of the mountain, a few hundred meters apart, have not been
covered with paving blocks. One of these would have been where the
Holy of Holies was situated. When the temple was burned and torn
down, it was so thoroughly destroyed that no two stones were left
standing one on the other. These stones were soon used in the
construction of other buildings in Jerusalem, so that the site the Romans
picked for their pagan temple sixty-five years later may not have been the
actual site of the Jewish temple (author).

20. For example, William E. Anderson, "Rapture? Sure … but when?" Green
Key Books, Holiday FL, 2003.

21. I used to think that seven years elapsed between the Rapture and the
Second Coming, to allow time to judge the works of Believers, until I
realized that there are only 217,730,000 seconds in seven years, hardly
enough time to properly judge those from all ages.

22. Marvin J. Rosenthal, <u>Zion's Fire</u>, Vol. 17, No.3, May-June, 2006, pg.20.

23. These numbers are based upon the present population of the earth, six
billion souls. The larger estimate is one-third of the whole earth; the lower
estimate is applicable if only one-fourth of the earth is affected, as in the
fourth seal (Rev. 6:8). Either is equally horrific.

24. On this occasion, the religious leaders told Jesus to tell the people not to
speak of Him as the Messiah. Jesus said that, if the people did not do this,
the stones would cry it out. This is not just a pious thought for us to
repeat today. It was the very last day of the 69th week of Daniel's
prophecy, and it HAD to be done.

25. "Although it may seem that we are having more earthquakes, earthquakes of magnitude 7.0 or greater have remained fairly constant throughout this [20th] century and, according to our records, have actually seemed to decrease in recent years." Source: http://earthquake.usgs.gov/learning/faq.php.

26. Ibid

27. Many fail to recognize this change in his point of reference and believe erroneously that there are two tribulation periods (verses nine and twenty-one), or at least that the last part of the tribulation will be worse than the first.

28. There are many speculations about the meaning of the vultures (or eagles). I offer this one for your consideration.

29. The other was in the Sermon on the Mount, when he said that he had come to fulfill the law and the prophets.

30. We remind the reader that the New Testament symbolizes Israel as an *Olive* tree, not a fig tree, into which the Church is grafted (Romans 11).

31. Although Israel gained control over the Temple Mount in 1967, they gave the PLO the authority to determine what could be done on the area.

32. The Seven Feasts of Israel, a pamphlet by Zola Levitt, copyright 1979.

33. For "wormwood," see Jeremiah 9:13-15, 23:15.

34. See the Bible text for a full and fascinating description of these "locusts."

35. The first satellite broadcast to consumers was by PBS on March 1, 1978. It would be some time before Jerusalem would have cameras to originate satellite pictures. Today, anyone with the right type cellular phone could instantly put these pictures on the Internet.

36. All the wicked dead will be raised at the end of the Millennium for judgment.

37. Oswald J. Smith, Is the Antichrist at Hand?—What of Mussolini, The Christian Alliance Publishing Company, New York, 1927.

38. To my thinking, Adolph Hitler, in his person and programs, came closest to fulfilling the prophecies of the Antichrist.

39. The ten nations agree to become a *coalition*, and when they agree to follow the leadership of the Antichrist, they become a *federation*.

40. He also revealed that kingdoms have spirit powers assigned to them, and that these spirit beings fight over the destiny of these countries.

41. For those who want to find them in Scripture, know that the USA has a fleet of ships based in Cyprus.

42. Frank Charles Thompson, The New CHAIN-REFERENCE BIBLE, Third Improved Edition 1934, B. B. Kirkbride Bible Co. Inc., Indianapolis Indiana, Condensed Cyclopedia of Topics and Texts, pp 246-249.

43. When the Jews rose up against the Greeks under the leadership of the Maccabees, it was necessary to sanctify the temple. The meager supply of pure oil for the lamps lasted far longer than could be expected. This is the miracle of Hanukkah that is celebrated by Jews each December.

44. www.en.wikipeda.org/wiki/Bar_Kokhba's_revolt.,

45. We have passed the 2000th anniversary of the death of Jesus, if the years are 360 days long. If they are true solar years, then the anniversary will come on April 14, 2032, approximately.

46. "Israel Claims Jerusalem" an address by President of Israel's Provisional State Council, Dr. Chaim Weizmann, December 1, 1948.

47. Sir Robert Anderson, The Coming Prince, Tenth Edition, Kregel Publications, Grand Rapids Michigan, 1986, chapter 10, Fulfillment of the Prophecy, pg. 119.

48. Tisha B'Av primarily commemorates the destruction of the first and second Temples, both of which were destroyed on the ninth of Av.

    Although this holiday is primarily meant to commemorate the destruction of the Temple, it is appropriate to consider on this day the many other tragedies of the Jewish people, many of which occurred on this day, most notably the expulsion of the Jews from Spain in 1492.

    Tisha B'Av is the culmination of a three week period of increasing mourning, beginning with the fast of the 17th of Tammuz, which commemorates the first breach in the walls of Jerusalem, before the First Temple was destroyed. During this three week period, weddings and other parties are not permitted, and people refrain from cutting their hair. From the first to the ninth of Av, it is customary to refrain from eating meat or drinking wine (except on the Shabbat) and from wearing new clothing.

    The restrictions on Tisha B'Av are similar to those on Yom Kippur: to refrain from eating and drinking (even water); washing, bathing, shaving or wearing cosmetics; wearing leather shoes; engaging in sexual relations; and studying Torah. Work in the ordinary sense of the word is also restricted. People who are ill need not fast on this day. Many of the traditional mourning practices are observed: people refrain from smiles, laughter and idle conversation, and sit on low stools. In synagogue, the book of Lamentations is read and mourning prayers are recited. The ark (cabinet where the Torah is kept) is draped in black.

    (copied from a website, origin not known)

49. A search of the internet will yield a wealth of information regarding the date on the Gregorian calendar, which actually did not exist until the 16th century. The most popular Hebrew—Gregorian calendar carries this note: "WARNING: Results for year 1752 C.E. and before may not be accurate. Hebcal does not take into account a correction of ten days that was introduced by Pope Gregory XIII known as the Gregorian Reformation." Another web site says that the Gregorian date August 2, 72 was August 4, 72 on the Julian calendar.

50. This may also be done using the Microsoft EXCEL software program, which is based on the Gregorian calendar. The results are the same.

51. Sir Robert Anderson, The Coming Prince, Tenth Edition, Kregel Publications, Grand Rapids Michigan, 1986, pg. 255.

52. Bernard Ramm, Protestant Biblical Interpretation, W.A. Wilde Company, 1950

Glossary

Abomination of Desolation—An interactive image of the Antichrist that will be placed in the Jewish temple in the middle of the 70th week of Daniel by the False Prophet. This idol will be so abhorrent to the Jews that they will cease to worship there (Dan. 9:27; 11:31; Matt. 24:15; 2 Thess. 2:4; Rev. 13:14-15).

Antichrist—A man who will be an evil spokesman for Satan in the latter days. He is known variously as "The ruler who will come" (Dan. 9:26), "A contemptible person who has not been given the honor of royalty" (Dan. 11:21), "The man of lawlessness" (2 Thess. 2:3; 1 John 2:18); "The Beast from the abyss" (Rev. 11:7); "The Beast from the Sea" (Rev. 13:1-8), and "The little horn" (Dan. 7:8, 11, 20-21).

Apostasy—A defection from the faith one has professed, specifically one said to take place before the Day of the Lord (Dan. 11:30; Matt. 24:10; 2 Thess. 2:3).

Armageddon—The final battle between Evil and Good that will take place at the end of the Tribulation (Joel 3:1-2; Zeph. 3:8; Rev. 12:12-16; 14:17-20; 19:11-21).

Babylon—1. A country Northeast of Israel. 2. The capitol city of the country of the same name. 3. A city emblematic of the evil world system that will be destroyed in the last days (Rev. 14:8; 16:19). Represented as a harlot (Rev. 17:1-18:24).

Beast from the Earth—See False Prophet

Beast from the Sea—See Antichrist

Beginning of Birth Pains—A term used by Jesus to describe those events that signal the last days (Matt. 24:7-8; Mark 13:8).

Bema Seat—The Judgment Seat of Christ. In ancient cultures, a place of judgment for the awarding of trophies in athletic contests. Extended to a final judgment of the works of the believers (2 Cor. 5:10). (see also Romans 14:10-12.)

Book of Life—A record of all the names of the elect, kept by God.
    Name written in the book from the foundation of world (Rev. 17:8).
    Possible to be blotted out (Exodus 32:30-32; Psalm 69:27; Rev. 3:5).
    Those whose names are written will be delivered from distress (Dan. 12:1; Rev. 21:27).
    Consequences for those whose names are NOT written (Rev. 13:8; 17:8; 20:15).
    Used as a basis for punishment (Rev. 20:12).

Bowl Judgments—A series of seven judgments which will be adminis-tered by God upon the wicked, comprising the final Wrath of God (Rev. 16:1-21).

Celestial Signs—A term to denote the signs that immediately precede the Rapture and the Day of the Lord (Matt. 24:29-31; Mark 13:24-27; Luke 21:25-28).

Church—With lower case, a local body of believers; an organization reg-istered with and recognized by the government.
Church Age—A period of time in which God deals primarily with the church, from Pentecost to the Rapture.

Covenant, 7-year—A treaty into which the Antichrist enters with Israel in the end times, initiating the 70th week of Daniel. In the middle of the period, he breaks the covenant by desecrating the Jewish temple in Jerusalem, starting the Tribulation.

Covenant, with Israel—God made an unconditional covenant with Abraham and his descendents, the Israelites involving their numbers, land, prosperity, and future kingdom. This is the covenant of Daniel 11:22, 30, 32 against which the Antichrist works.

Day of Christ—A term used by Paul exclusively in the epistle to the Philippians, synonymous with the Rapture,

Day of God—A term used by Paul, synonymous with the Day of the Lord (2 Peter 3:10-12).

Day of the Lord—A biblical term for the final punishment of the wicked and restoration of creation.

Dispensations—Sequential time periods that some theologians use to designate the different ways which God deals with mankind in each. The age in which we now live has been described by contemporaries as the "Age of Grace" or the "Church Age."

Dispensationalist—One who believes that God deals with the world in periods of time called dispensations. In particular, the dispensations are believed by some to be of 1000 years each.

Eschatology—The system and study of end-time prophecy.

False Prophet—The ally of the Antichrist who exalts and promotes him in the world (Dan. 9:27; 11:31; Rev. 13:11-17; 16:13; 19:20). See also Beast from the Earth.

Gabriel—An angel who delivers God's messages to His prophets (Dan. 8:16; 9:21; Luke 1:19, 26).

Harlot, Babylon—Symbol of the evil world system. In Revelation 17, found riding on a beast representing Satan's organization (Rev. 17:1, 15, 16; 19:2).

Heads, as used in symbolic prophecy—Representative of men, empires, kings, or hills. For example, Revelation 17:9-10

Hermeneutics—The discipline of Bible study.

Horns—In prophecy, symbolic of men of leadership. For example, Revelation 17:12

Imminent return of Christ—The doctrine that Christ may return at any moment for His church.

Judgment Seat of Christ—A judgment of works of the believer. See Bema Seat

KJV—King James Version of the Bible.

Literalist—One who believes in the literal interpretation of the Bible. See Hermeneutics.

Little Horn—In Daniel, both the future coming Antichrist of chapter seven, said to arise from the ten kings in the last days (Daniel 7:8), and in chapter eight, Antiochus Epiphanes, who came from the Greek empire (Daniel 8:9).

Mark of the Beast—A visible mark that the False Prophet will have engraved in the forehead or the right hand of the person who will worship the Antichrist. The mark will be either the name of the Antichrist or the number of his name, 666. The citizens of the land over which the Antichrist rules will not be able to buy or sell without the mark (Rev. 13:16-18).

Michael—An archangel charged with watching over the nation of Israel (Dan. 12:1).

Midtribulation—Regarding the timing of the Rapture, to take place in the middle of the Tribulation.

Marriage Feast of the Lamb—A wedding feast to which many are invited, honoring the marriage of Christ to the church (Matt. 22:1-14 (parable); 25:1-13 (parable); Rev. 19:7-9).

Millennium—From the Greek milli (one thousand) and annum (year), the one thousand year period also known as the Kingdom (Rev. 20:1-4).

NASB—New American Standard Bible.

NIV—New International Version of the Bible.

Olivet Discourse—A term given to the monologue of Jesus to His disciples on the Mount of Olives a few days before His crucifixion, regarding the end times (Matt. 24:3-25:26; Mark 13:3-35; Luke 21:3-33).

Parable—A short story told to illustrate a single truth.

Partial Rapture—A rapture theory based upon the belief that only the part of the church who are looking for the return of Christ will be taken when Christ returns to the earth. The remainder stays on earth during the tribulation, to join Christ at the end of the tribulation.

Post-tribulation: Spoken of the timing of the Rapture, to take place after the Tribulation.

Pre-millennial: Spoken of the timing of the Rapture, to take place before the Millennium.

Pre-tribulation: Spoken of the timing of the Rapture, to take place before the Tribulation.

Pre-Wrath—An end time theory that believes that the church will be raptured at some time after the Abomination and revelation of the

Antichrist, but before the Wrath of God is administered upon the wicked.

Prophecy (noun)—Prediction of things in the future.

Prophesy (verb)—to predict the future.

Rapture—The event in which living saints are taken out of the earth supernaturally to meet Christ in the air. Closely associated with the resurrection of the saintly dead. The word is not found in Scripture (1Cor. 15:51-53; 1 Thess. 4:13-18).

Restrainer—The entity that has been holding back Satan from exercising his full power on the earth (2 Thess. 2:2-12).

Resurrection—The raising of a person from the dead. Scripture teaches that there will be two general resurrections; the righteous at Christ's coming, and the wicked after the Millennium (Dan. 12:1-2; Rev. 20:5-6).

Seal Judgments—The series of seven judgments in Revelation (Rev. 5:1-8:5).

Simile—A figure of speech characterized by the words as, like as, etc. comparing an object to another.

Seventy Weeks of Daniel—Prophesied in Daniel 9:24-27 as seventy times seven years of time. The term "week" is not found in the prophecy; rather "seven".

Seventieth Week of Daniel—The last of the seventy weeks of Daniel, referenced separately because it is future to us.

Sheep and Goat Judgment—A judgment found in Matthew 25:31-46, in which the nations of the earth are categorized as either good or bad, based upon their works toward God's people.

Thunder Judgments—A series of judgments in the Revelation which are not described in detail (Rev. 10:3-4).

Time of Jacob's Trouble—A prophesied time of unprecedented persecution of Israel, beginning with the abomination of desolation and continuing through the restoration of the earth. A time when Israel will turn again to God, and to

Jesus as Messiah (Jer. 30:6-7).

Tribulation: A period of unusual stress and persecution on earth, never seen before nor ever to come after (Dan. 12:1; Matt. 24:21).

Trumpet Judgments—A series of judgments in Revelation. At the last trumpet, also called the trumpet of God, the church will be raptured (Rev. 8:6-11:19).

Type (n.)—an object representing a more intensive thing (also called an anti-type) to come later. The type has most of the characteristics and nature of the anti-type it foretells.

Wedding Feast—See Marriage Feast of the Lamb.

Witnesses, Two—The two men who will act as God's spokesmen in the tribulation. See Revelation 11:3-13.

Wrath of God—A wide variety of meanings in Scripture of God's anger, from a passive permission to allow sin to run its course (Romans 1), to the final act of vindication specifically in the end times. Shown first in the sixth seal (Rev. 6:12-17; 14:17-20; 16:1-21).

Scripture Index

8:20-23	59
10:9-10	102

1 CORINTHIANS

1:8	61, 67
3:13-15	103
5:5	60, 61, 62
11:30	103
14:22	168
15:20-23	52
15:23-24	53
15:24	60
15:51-54	53, 95
15:52	61, 97

2 CORINTHIANS

1:14	60, 61
12:20	67

GALATIANS

5:20	67

EPHESIANS

5:6	67

PHILIPPIANS

1:6	61
1:10	61
2:16	61

COLOSSIANS

3:6	67
3:8	67

1 THESSALONIANS

1:10	67
2:16	67
4:14	61, 97
4:16	52, 97

4:16-17	53
4:17	97
5:1-4	57
5:2	60, 62
5:3	52
5:4	62
5:4-6	100, 158
5:9	67
5:20-21	148

2 THESSALONIANS

2:1-4	56
2:2	60, 62
2:3	43, 91, 127, 129, 138
2:3-4	42, 44
2:3-8	130
2:4	129
2:4-9	139
2:6-7	142
2:6-12	43
2:8	128
2:9-12	138
2:9	47

1 TIMOTHY

4:1	43

HEBREWS

11:27	67

1 PETER

1:7	62
2:2-3	166

2 PETER

3:7	79
3:8	152
3:10	60, 91